WASHINGTON'S
MOUNT RAINIER
A Centennial Celebration
NATIONAL PARK

WASHINGTON'S

MOUNT RAINIER NATIONAL PARK

A Centennial Celebration

TEXT BY TIM McNULTY ◆ PHOTOGRAPHS BY PAT O'HARA

THE MOUNTAINEERS

Published by
The Mountaineers
1001 SW Klickitat Way, Suite 201
Seattle, WA 98134

Text by Tim McNulty
Color photographs by Pat O'Hara
©1998 by Tim McNulty and Pat O'Hara

First edition, 1998

Published simultaneously in Great Britain by Cordee,
3a DeMontfort Street, Leicester, England, LE1 7HD

Manufactured in Singapore by Imago/Star Standard
Industries, Ltd.

Edited by Cynthia Newman Bohn
Map and illustrations by Jim Hays
Cover and book design by Alice C. Merrill

Black and white photos courtesy: Mount Rainier Archives
Project, National Archives and Records
Administration, Seattle, pp. 46, 54, 63; Washington
State Historical Society, Tacoma, pp. 39, 44 (right),
45, 49, 51; Mount Rainier Archives, National Park
Service, pp. 33, 44 (left), 57, 58, 60, 65; The
Mountaineers Archive, Special Collections,
University of Washington Libraries, 53.

Cover: The mountain from White River valley
Half-title page: Mountain and cloud, morning light
Frontispiece: Reflection Lake, early autumn
Contents page: The mountain, Little Tahoma, and
    lenticular cloud
Pages 32-33: Sunset Amphitheater and the Puyallup
    and Tahoma glaciers
Pages 68-69: Emmons Glacier and Little Tahoma
    Peak, Mount Saint Helens in distance
Pages 88-89: Grandfather redcedars, Grove of the
    Patriarchs

Library of Congress Cataloging-in-Publication Data
McNulty, Tim.
    Washington's Mount Rainier National Park :
a centennial celebration / text by Tim McNulty ;
photographs by Pat O'Hara.
        p.   cm.
    Includes bibliographical references and index
    ISBN 0-89886-582-4 (cloth); 0-89886-621-9
    (paper)
    1. Mount Rainier National Park (Wash.)—History.
2. Natural history—Washington (State)—Mount
Rainier National Park.
I. O'Hara, Pat. II. Title.
F897.R2M45 1998
979.7'782—dc21

Contents

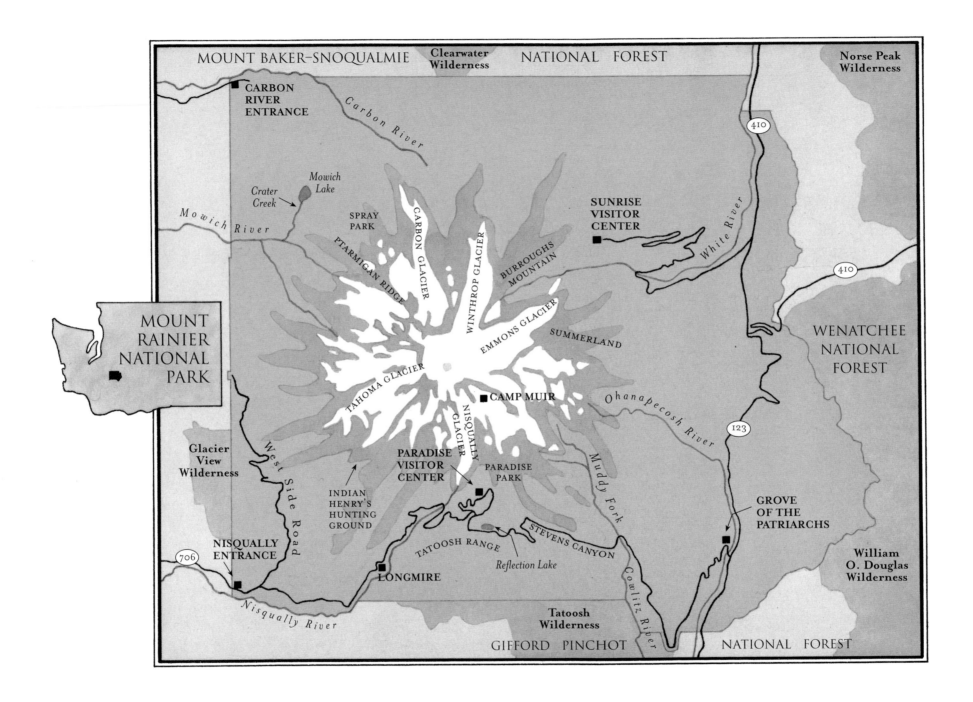

MOUNT BAKER–SNOQUALMIE   **Clearwater Wilderness**   NATIONAL FOREST   **Norse Peak Wilderness**

■ **CARBON RIVER ENTRANCE**

Carbon River

Mowich River

Crater Creek   *Mowich Lake*

SPRAY PARK

PTARMIGAN RIDGE

CARBON GLACIER

WINTHROP GLACIER

BURROUGHS MOUNTAIN

EMMONS GLACIER

SUMMERLAND

SUNRISE VISITOR CENTER ■

White River

410

410

WENATCHEE NATIONAL FOREST

MOUNT RAINIER NATIONAL PARK

TAHOMA GLACIER

■ **CAMP MUIR**

NISQUALLY GLACIER

Ohanapecosh River

123

PARADISE VISITOR CENTER

Paradise Park ■

Glacier View Wilderness

West Side Road

INDIAN HENRY'S HUNTING GROUND

TATOOSH RANGE

Reflection Lake

STEVENS CANYON

Muddy Fork

GROVE OF THE PATRIARCHS → ■

William O. Douglas Wilderness

706

NISQUALLY ENTRANCE ■

■ **LONGMIRE**

Nisqually River

Tatoosh Wilderness

Cowlitz River

GIFFORD PINCHOT   NATIONAL FOREST

FOREWORD

Mount Rainier presides over our region as a gentle spirit. Occasionally, over the ages, this benign mountain blows its top with a fury that radically changes the surrounding landscape. The last time Rainier erupted, few humans witnessed its massive destruction, or were affected by the years it took to heal the land.

We Northwesterners today are continually inspired by Mount Rainier's presence. On blue-sky days when the mountain shows its freshly whitened face, I hear the common greeting, "Have you seen the mountain today?" In elevators, at the office or in a restaurant, between friends or strangers, this mantra rejuvenates the soul and adds brightness to the day.

Indian tribes for centuries revered Rainier, but respecting it or fearing its spirit, never trod on its upper slopes. Early explorers instead sought to conquer this magnificent mountain. Soon two stood on top, followed by a trickle, and then today's flood of climbers, who revel in the experience and are proud of their accomplishment, but they have never conquered Rainier.

I remember every moment of my climb of Mount Rainier. The warm, sunny trek to Camp Muir followed by afternoon sunbathing gave no hint of tomorrow's adventure. We crawled out of sleeping bags at 1:00 A.M., carefully roped up and donned crampons. As we started the climb I looked up at a star-filled sky and felt the enormity of the universe as never before. Dawn revealed crevasses beckoning on all sides and the dazzling white crest of Rainier seemed impossibly far away. Each slowly plodding step brought the top closer until the last glorious moment when there was no more "up." We surveyed most of Washington State and Rainier's sister volcanoes, then turned to the crater whose steaming vents reminded us that this mountain was not dead, but only sleeping. The trip down was a fast, joyous journey to Paradise. As I gazed back at the

Reflection in mountain tarn, Chinook Pass

mountain, I experienced a renewed bond with nature which returns every time I see the mountain.

As population grew near Puget Sound, entrepreneurs sought to tame this unruly territory. Trees were an impediment to farming and settlement and were an early cash crop. Recreation required roads, hotels, trails, ski areas, and even tramways. Rainier wasn't immune from this onslaught of civilization. Roads slowly crept up its slopes and trails stitched mountain meadows together. Tourists followed and the tramp of millions of footprints devastated fragile wildflowers.

Fortunately, wise early citizens recognized the precious heritage of Rainier and began the long and continuing task of protection. National Park status, wilderness designation, and control over access and climbing all helped.

We long ago ceased trying to conquer Rainier but are now in mortal danger of loving it to death. Thousands of climbers and millions of visitors seek sustenance from this remarkable place. But we are only transients and our children and grandchildren deserve to experience Rainier in its natural grandeur. If they are to learn the teachings of the mountain, we must not use up its fragile beauty.

Wilderness protection is designed as a window to the past so each generation can view our earth as it was before human alteration. The regulations necessary to protect wilderness sometimes seem onerous. Some believe too much land is preserved, but wilderness once destroyed cannot be regained. We must not bankrupt the bank account of our natural heritage.

Read this extraordinary account of Mount Rainier and the people who have revered, assaulted, coveted, enjoyed, and protected its beauty. Each picture tells of the richness and variety of nature's bounty. The text reminds us of our responsibility to protect that bounty. If this book leads you to the mountain, you will return awed by its majesty, invigorated by its changing seasons, and dedicated to preserving its integrity.

Enjoy!

— *Daniel J. Evans*
Governor of Washington, 1965–1977

A CENTURY OF RESOURCE STEWARDSHIP

Looking through Tim McNulty and Pat O'Hara's centennial celebration of Mount Rainier National Park, I was reminded once more of the beauty and grandeur of this, our nation's fifth national park. And I'm reminded also of the pleasure it is to serve as its superintendent. Even as I sat reviewing the book on a blustery day on the Oregon coast, the author and photographer's salute to Mount Rainier brought me right back to the majesty of that incredible landscape.

From a favorite perch overlooking the pounding surf, I traveled back with the authors, feeling the reverence and awe in which generations of Native Americans held the mountain, as well as the challenge and adventure sought there by European explorers and settlers. The mountain inspired those adventurers and moved them to work for its protection. John Muir, an early visitor to Mount Rainier and one of the fathers of the American conservation movement, described the mountain as the noblest of the Cascade volcanoes and urged that it be designated a national park and "guarded while yet its bloom is on." His call for preservation of the mountain and its surrounding forests was soon joined by prominent scientists, local newspapers, and mountain clubs. During the last year of the nineteenth century, Mount Rainier National Park was born.

McNulty and O'Hara's familiarity with and affection for the park shine through every page of this book. Their words and images evoke the sights, sounds, and smells of the ancient forests, flower fields, rivers, and glaciers of Mount Rainier. Through their work, I recall my own excursions into the mountain wilderness over the years, and I savor once more the refreshed perspective and renewed appreciation for nature's blessings with which I always return. I find myself thankful for the vision of those who worked one

Spring melt, Tipsoo Lake

~

**Bracken fern and
vine maple**

hundred years ago to preserve this natural treasure for future generations.

As I look back over the park's first century, I think of the early rangers and naturalists who worked to protect the natural wonders Congress saw fit to preserve, and who helped generations of visitors appreciate and enjoy them. Owen Tomlinson served a long and distinguished career as superintendent in the 1920s and 1930s. Appointed by Stephen Mather, the first director of the National Park Service, he was instrumental in building a professional ranger corps at the park. Both John Rutter and Daniel Tobin, superintendents in the 1960s and 1970s, went on to serve as regional directors for the Park Service. In 1924 Floyd Schmoe became Mount Rainier's first park naturalist. An author as well as a citizen activist, Floyd recently celebrated his own centennial—well ahead of the park. Another fine naturalist, Dale Thompson, retired from the park to become an accomplished Northwest wildlife artist. Among the many rangers who have stood out in their service to the park and the public, Bill Butler deserves special mention. He led

countless search and rescue missions during his more than thirty-year association with Mount Rainier, and he received national recognition for his efforts.

The work of these and so many other men and women, both inside and outside the Park Service, has insured our continued enjoyment of this magnificent mountain wilderness. It has been said that the "National Parks are America's greatest idea." As we at Mount Rainier National Park prepare for its second century of resource stewardship, we draw on the vision of early park advocates, the dedication of its protectors over the years, and the professionalism of our own resource managers to maintain that magnificence into the twenty-first century and beyond. It's a big job, and one that we cannot do alone. But we have the visionaries of the past to guide us, and the gratitude of future generations as our reward.

—*William J. Briggle*
Superintendent, Mount Rainier National Park

〜 Western redcedar and autumn vine maples,
Falls Creek

A WILD AND RESTLESS BEAUTY

The massive, ice-clad form of Mount Rainier lifts over the shores of the inland sea and the high deserts to the east like a visitation from another age. Its rivers of ice evoke a time when humans first came to this glacier-torn landscape; its lava walls are inscribed with a text of the earth's violent renewal. Yet its presence holds a gift to the present and a promise to the future.

The mountain warps our senses of time and scale. It rises isolated and immense over the older weathered hills of the Cascades. Its wild beauty dazzles. Its nearness beckons. It draws us up to its rugged slopes like moths to a snowlit lamp.

For more than a hundred miles in any direction Mount Rainier is the dominant landform on the horizon, and its hold over our imaginations in the Northwest is almost mystical. It is a symbol of pristine wildness close upon our urban doorsteps, a reminder of the immediacy of the earth's formative power. It is a recreational Mecca and spiritual retreat. And a landscape both harsh and heartrending in its beauty.

At dawn the mountain's shoulders gather a first pale scrim of light and slowly stir the region to life. Its rough contours fade in morning sunlight, and on summer afternoons the mountain sometimes hovers

above the lowland haze, disembodied and adrift. Evening light sharpens the amphitheaters and cliffs of the upper slopes as shadows claim the mountain from below, softening canyons and ridges and settling the massif back upon its darkened range, luminescent and still.

In winter, the mountain can disappear for days or weeks as clouds blanket the lowlands and rain runs in sheets down city streets. When the weather breaks and the mountain emerges, robed in snow and brilliant in slant winter sunlight, it presides almost godlike above the welter and buzz of our lowland scuttlings, gracing the region with an otherworldly air.

A century ago Americans drew a rough boundary around the mountain, its meadows, waterfalls, and fringe of lowland forest, and designated Mount Rainier our country's fifth national park. Since then, millions of visitors have traveled to its slopes to take in its wild and restless beauty, as they will for generations to come. That's the mission and the promise of a national park—a promise our culture holds sacred. But we are not the first to have held the mountain in awe, or to have journeyed to its slopes for a kind of sustenance. Long before Europeans named and mapped and measured it, the mountain held sway over the lives and imaginations of the region's earliest inhabitants.

The mountain in winter

The archaeological record shows evidence of human use of the mountain going back at least two thousand years. Cave shelters, camps, and at least one quarry site for stone tools speak of a long and intimate human presence. For the first people to dwell in its realm the great white peak, like the rest of nature, was imbued with spirit. In early myths and legends it is possessed of an unsettling mix of superhuman powers and human passions, and capable of fiery shifts in mood. Harsh experience taught native people that the mountain which dominated their horizon could change suddenly from a nurturing to a demonic presence. And the stories that have come down to us reflect the mountain's complex moods.

To the Nisqually people she was *Tacobet,* "nourishing breast" or "the place where waters begin." A Nisqually tale tells us that Tacobet was once a wife, mother, and provider. When she grew too large for her husband and family in their crowded home in the Olympic Mountains, she moved across the great Whulge where there was ample room. Tacobet came with gifts. Her milky rivers brought salmon to the people. Berries, roots, and game were plentiful on her open slopes. But in her solitude she grew gigantic and assumed the disposition and appetite of a monster. Transformed, she devoured anyone who came near. It took Doquebuth the Changer himself to subdue her and return her to her nurturing ways. But the volatile hag lies slumbering close beneath the surface. A similar legend from the Skokomish people depicts the mountain as wife to the warrior Dosewallips. She quarreled jealously with her husband's other wife and eventually became so angry she left him for an outpost across the sound. Even from that distance the wives continued to bicker, bellowing and hurling lightning bolts back and forth, and frightening the people huddled in their villages below.

These legends reflect more than a passing familiarity with the mountain's destructive nature, a darker side of the Cascade volcanoes' beauty that was made starkly clear with the 1980 eruption of Mount Saint

Monkeyflowers and moss, Sunbeam Creek

Helens. Other Native American stories reflect an intimacy with the mountain and its ways that is almost geologic in scope. Many legends tell of a lake on the mountain's summit, a phenomenon most geologists consider plausible. In one story a young Puyallup man traveled to the summit lake on a spirit quest. He made the long difficult ascent using "five elk-horn wedges to cut steps in the snow and ice." After the young seeker camped for the night and cleansed himself in the summit lake, Tacobet spoke to him. She told him he would live to be an old man, then she issued a dire prediction. Years later when the man died, the prophecy came true. The mountain burst open and her summit lake surged into the valleys below, sweeping away forests and villages in its path and leaving the Puyallup Valley littered with pieces of herself. This story was first recorded in the 1920s, but it proved strangely accurate decades later. That is when geologists found the flat valley around Orting and Sumner to have been deposited by a massive mudflow that swept down from the mountain more than five hundred years ago.

Our modern association with the mountain reaches back just two centuries, and in many ways Mount Rainier remains a landscape still fresh with discovery. A mere century and three-quarters has lapsed since the first scientific exploration of Mount Rainier, less than a century and a half since the first attempt on its summit. Only at the close of the nineteenth century did a handful of visionaries in the booming frontier settlements of Puget Sound join efforts with national scientific and conservation societies and succeed in preserving Mount Rainier as a national park.

Since then, the population of the Puget Sound region has increased a thousandfold. Highways have swallowed rail lines and wagon roads, and cities have pushed from coastal areas to the foothills. For a population approaching 3.3 million, Mount Rainier National Park is now within a three-hour drive. Its forests, meadows, and snow-shrouded slopes attract more than 2 million visitors each year. The mountain's role in the recreational life of the region has grown proportionally as well. While Mount Rainier remains a mountaineering challenge for thousands of climbers, it is also a summer and winter playground,

Emergent wetland, Ohanapecosh Valley

a place to contemplate and learn about the natural world, a quick escape from the city, and a revered spiritual retreat. More than any other wilderness national park, Mount Rainier is a nearby destination where a growing urban population can step back, however briefly, into a world of timeless beauty and savor a landscape little changed from the one that inspired those early storytellers as they huddled around their winter fires.

And to the continued delight of all of us who find ourselves irrevocably drawn to it, Mount Rainier is among the most stunningly beautiful and diverse of all our national parks.

As early as 1894, Bailey Willis of the Geological Society of America described Mount Rainier as "an arctic island in a temperate zone." It is an image that still rings true. As the climate warmed and valley glaciers and the great Cordilleran ice sheet receded at the close of the Pleistocene, habitats for arctic alpine plants and animals disappeared across broad regions in the Northwest. With its high, open slopes extending thousands of feet above the surrounding mountains, Mount Rainier became an island refuge for a number of alpine species. Today the mountain is home to a host of alpine plants; many of these are found only in the Pacific Northwest and many others are rare enough to have been proposed for threatened or endangered listing in Washington. Three are endemic species—survivors of once-larger populations or pioneers forging new lines of evolution—found nowhere else in the world.

The park's vast elevational range, from 1,700 to over 14,000 feet, offers habitats for a wonderful diversity of plant and animal life—from the low-elevation old-growth forests of the river valleys through dense, montane forests of the mountain slopes to extravagant subalpine parklands and rocky alpine gardens. The alpine zone alone, that sere, windy, and exposed terrain which lies above the highest growth of trees on the mountain, extends from between 6,000 and 7,000 feet to an upper end close to 11,000 feet—more than twice the extent of alpine areas on other Northwest peaks.

Spreading phlox in snow

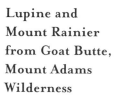

Lupine and
Mount Rainier
from Goat Butte,
Mount Adams
Wilderness

19

20

◦ **Winter meadows, Wahpenayo Peak,**
Tatoosh Range

At 14,410 feet, Mount Rainier is the tallest of Cascade volcanoes, and with a footprint of over 100 square miles, it is also the largest. Its great height lifts and cools a steady onshore flow from the Pacific, weaving warm blankets of ocean moisture into tattered quilts and ragged scarves of stormcloud. Between November and March storms dump more than 50 feet of snow on the mountain's upper slopes (as much as 90 feet in a record year), feeding a summit ice cap and a radial network of glaciers 34 square miles in extent. Rainier's prodigious glaciers constitute the largest single-peak system in the United States outside Alaska and hold more ice than all of the other Cascade volcanoes combined. In many ways, Rainier's glaciers are its crowning feature. As an early twentieth-century topographer observed, they "vie in magnitude and in splendor with the most boasted glaciers of the Alps." The mountain's ice streams flow hundreds of feet in depth and push farther down into valley forests than any others in the contiguous states. Over a relatively short span of time they have scraped and sculpted the mountain from the graceful contours of a youthful

stratovolcano, suggestive of Mount Fuji or the pre-eruption Mount Saint Helens, into its present broad and truncated shape. Rainier's glaciers are finely calibrated monitors of climate change, and they play a pivotal role in the region's industry, agriculture, and fisheries. Their meltwaters feed five major river systems, which churn and cascade through the park's unbroken forests and eventually merge with Puget Sound and the Columbia River, providing miles of productive salmon habitat as well as serving a portion of the region's irrigation and hydroelectric needs. And for climbers from across the country, they are a surrogate Himalaya.

Come summer, all that snowfall translates into well-watered mountain meadows, and Mount Rainier National Park is renowned for its exquisite subalpine parklands. The old Salish name for the splendid meadows of Paradise Park on the mountain's south side is *Saghalie Illahe,* "heavenly place" or "land of peace," evoking a spiritual realm apart from the hardships of life below. Their current name, bestowed by a member of the Longmire family in 1885, carries that

Paradise in winter

21

earlier vision into our culture today. Writer and naturalist John Muir called the meadowlands of Paradise "extravagantly beautiful" when he visited the mountain in 1888; contemporary writer and seasoned mountain traveler Harvey Manning praises them as "unsurpassed anywhere in the Cascades."

The park's subalpine meadows encircle the mountain's upper slopes like a flowery bracelet. Heavy snows dampen forest growth at upper elevations, and the mountain's deep, ash-deposited soils, amply watered during the short growing season, bring forth luxurious wildflower displays. In July when snow blankets recede into remnant patches and creeks swell with snowmelt, the meadows erupt into snowy fields of avalanche lilies. Later in summer they are awash in waves of blue lupine. Blooming cycles progress in an impressionist's array of hues: golden arnica, scarlet paintbrush, the late-blooming blues of gentian— a color that often meets the autumn blush of huckleberry leaves. The gardens are broken by islandlike copses and ribbons of subalpine trees—firs, mountain hemlocks, Alaska yellow-cedars. To hike the

meadowlands of Paradise or Spray Park, Summerland or Sunrise, is to discover a mosaic of meadow and high forest that is among the most stunning in North America.

Everywhere you look in this mountain world, the hand of winter has written boldly over the landscape. Subalpine trees huddle in dense clusters for protection from winter storms; seedlings that venture out into open meadows are likely to be pruned back by icy winds. The trees that have adapted to these harsh conditions are generally spirelike and small in stature; their short, flexible limbs yield to shed the weight of winter snows. The lower limbs or "skirts" of some subalpine trees take root beneath the spring snow and send up shoots of new trees. Young trees laid flat by the downward creep of snowpack burst upright during the warming days of spring.

Beyond the upper limit of tree growth a few hardy plants hug the rocky ground in the lee of stones and outcrops or hunker in low snowbound depressions. These tough alpine cushion and matlike plants endure sub-freezing conditions and summer

Old Douglas-firs

droughts as they gather bits of soil and nutrients blown in by the wind. Mount Rainier's alpine plants are exceptionally hardy and well adapted to the severe conditions that prevail above treeline. They have adapted to everything their harsh volcanic environments have to offer—everything, that is, but us and our lug-soled boots. Over the past century our numbers on the mountain have leapfrogged off the scale of evolutionary change. Only by our continued awareness and concern can we insure that the rich natural legacy we currently enjoy will be there for those who follow us.

Because of its sheer mass Mount Rainier has the effect of a small mountain range. By interrupting the flow of prevailing weather systems the mountain creates its own rainshadow. A microcosm of the arid rainshadow cast by the Cascade Mountains over eastern Washington, Rainier's eastern slopes receive considerably less rain and snow than the rest of the mountain. This results in a longer and drier growing season for Burroughs Mountain and Yakima Park. The same prevailing winds have deposited pumice

eruptions on the mountain's east side as well. The combination of well-drained soils and droughty summer conditions results in unique plant communities that include herbs, shrubs, and trees more often found on the dry east slope of the Cascades. Rainier's rainshadow is also known to draw discriminating

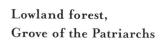

**Lowland forest,
Grove of the Patriarchs**

23

Mountain, river, and
forest, White River
valley

visitors from the west side. When Paradise is lost in damp clouds, Sunrise is often bathed in sunlight.

Farther down the mountain's slopes, the park's forest communities echo the give and take of weather and topography. The moss-covered hemlock and Sitka spruce forests of the Carbon River valley in the northwest corner of the park seem as lush and verdant as the Olympics' famed temperate rain forests, while the open, fire-influenced Douglas-fir stands of the Ohanapecosh Valley in the southeast corner present a forest of an entirely different character. From the time the park was first proposed, its forest stands were praised as exceptional in a land of outstanding forests. More recently Jerry Franklin, the dean of old-growth forest ecology in the Northwest, described them as among the most impressive in the world. As clearcutting has all but eliminated old-growth forests on lands outside parks and protected areas, Mount Rainier's lowland forests have become even more of a treasure. As our understanding of the complex interrelationships within the forest increases, and surrounding land managers look to restore forest ecosys-

tems on logged lands, the park's forests may serve as both a working model and an invaluable genetic reserve for reintroducing species and biological processes into younger forests. In the meantime Mount Rainier's 200 square miles of trees will continue to provide critical habitats for a range of forest-dwelling wildlife. And the park's ancient groves will inspire visitors for centuries to come.

LIKE MANY NEW ARRIVALS TO THE PACIFIC NORTHWEST, I was captured by the mountain the moment I saw it. That was almost thirty years ago, and it has held me in its spell ever since. I would be hard pressed to imagine the Northwest without Mount Rainier—any more than without salmon, or cedar, or rain. Though I settled on the west side of Puget Sound I felt compelled to pay homage to the region's reigning icon. One of my first mountain outings in the Northwest was a "circumambulation" of the mountain —in the tradition of pilgrims in India and Tibet. I was innocent of local etiquette toward the mountain, but I read that the Yakama people knew the peak as Tahoma, "the great mountain which gives thunder and lightning." That sounded good to me.

I was also unaware of the valiant but doomed effort the city fathers of Tacoma mounted to change the mountain's name to Mount Tacoma. A generic Salish term, Tacoma or Tahoma is also the name for any snow-covered peak. Loosely translated it means "the Mountain." Appropriately, Rainier remains "the Mountain" in common Northwest parlance today. The name captures the intimate familiarity of those earlier names of Mount Rainier (if not their literal translations), and in its own way restores a "native" identity to the region's most potent symbol.

The timing for my pilgrimage around the mountain could have been better. The winter of 1971–72 dumped record snows on Mount Rainier, and by late July few of the mountain's trails had melted free. Low clouds and rain kept the peak hidden for most of a week during my initial audience with the thunder maker. I don't recall actually seeing the upper snowfields and glaciers, but the mountain's awesome power and presence were in evidence all around me: in churning glacier-fed rivers and steep mountain forests sluiced by avalanche tracks, and in the chill icy breath of snowfields that whistled through my camp at night. Trudging through the unbroken snowpack, crossing ridges lost in clouds, I didn't complete my hike around Tahoma that year, but I returned often in the years that followed to hike and climb and camp—in fair weather as well as miserable. To love a mountain, I soon learned, is to accept it as it is, don rain gear and gaiters, and be ready to adjust your plans.

In the 1970s I began to venture up a few of Rainier's climbing routes. I witnessed the impacts people like me were having on alpine plant communities, and I wrote in support of Park Service efforts to limit use on parts of the mountain to protect fragile areas. Later I wrote letters and testified before congressional committees to help secure wilderness protection for roadless national forest lands adjoining the park. In the mid-1980s I returned with my friend and collaborator, photographer Pat O'Hara to work on one of our earliest projects together, a book exploring the beauty and diversity of Mount Rainier National Park.

American River valley, morning light

26

We backpacked in to mountain lakes, hiked up river valleys, and visited countless forests, waterfalls, and parks. Once we were caught in a late-season snowstorm high on the mountain's northern flank. On another trip we tracked a band of elk on their fall migration out of the park. There were hikes when the weather was so uncooperative Pat never unpacked his camera. But on these trips I honed the fine art of listening to the mountain, tuning in to the nuances of the mountain's character—the chatter of juncos beneath subalpine firs, the cadenced fall of a distant creek, or the wing-chuff of a passing raven—while Pat composed with camera and lens and waited for the perfect light.

Pat's involvement with Mount Rainier goes back much further than mine. A Northwesterner by birth, Pat grew up in the presence of the mountain, and its image proved a touchstone throughout his youth. On clear days, he recalls, Mount Rainier owned the horizon across Lake Washington. Pat made regular trips to the park as a young boy with his family in the 1950s, and the mountain provided his earliest encounters with the wild. He remembers hearing of a black bear visiting the old cabins at Ohanapecosh Hot Springs where his family stayed one year, and making up his mind to find it. "I was no more than six or seven," he recalls. "Early one morning, without telling my parents, I ventured out into the woods in search of the bear." What's more surprising: he found it, curled up asleep at the base of a large old-growth tree. It was a big bear, but tucked among the roots of the huge tree, it seemed tiny. "That was an incredible moment for me," he remembers years later. "It was my first real sense of the vastness and mystery of wild nature." The glimpse was a brief one; the bear woke at Pat's approach and trundled up the hillside, but the magic of the encounter burned itself into Pat's imagination and kindled a lifelong desire to explore wild nature that informs his work today.

As a photographer, Pat focused his early work on unprotected wildlands in his native state. His first book, *Washington Wilderness: The Unfinished Work,* written by Harvey Manning and published by The Mountaineers, was instrumental in the passage of legislation that secured wilderness protection for more than a million

acres of the state's finest wildlands. Pat hiked and photographed then-unprotected wild country adjoining Mount Rainier National Park for the book, as well as the park itself. He remembers the mountain looming like a sentinel from the high points of nearly every wilderness area he visited. The mountain continues to exert an irrevocable pull on Pat's imagination. He carries on a family tradition by returning to the park with his wife, Tina, and daughter Trisha, and the mountain continues to inspire some of Pat's most striking and enduring work.

*I*T'S A SUNNY WEEKDAY IN LATE JULY AND I'M IN THE process of initiating a family tradition of my own. I've come to the mountain with my wife, Mary, our daughter Caitlin, and her steadfast mountain companion Hiking Bear to stroll the wildflower gardens of Paradise and hope for an unobstructed glimpse of the giant. It will be Caitlin's first close-up encounter, and she has laced up her hiking boots and tucked an emergency ration of gummy bears into her small day pack. The parking lot is full of cars and buses, and we

29

join a decidedly international crowd as we start up the trail to Panorama Point. Within a half-hour's walk we've left most of the congestion behind, and we continue upward through sweet-smelling fields of lupine just beginning its midsummer spread over the open slopes. Here and there we find the meadows lit with bright flames of paintbrush or softened by cottony tufts of bistort. Higher up, yellow glacier lilies and white avalanche lilies crowd the margins of melting snowbanks, and pale western anemones, red monkey-flowers, and delicate purple shooting stars trace the courses of snowmelt streams. Bees hum among the heather blooms and yellow-pine chipmunks panhandle shamelessly along trailside rest spots. A marmot sprawls over a sentry rock, apparently asleep at his post, and gray jays swoop from tree to tree as if expecting a tithe.

We pass families with kids along the trail, and seniors who inevitably stop to compliment Caitlin's bear. We chat with a group from a summer camp, and a family who lives near the base of the mountain. Soon, the frozen cascade of the Nisqually Glacier appears below us, broken and rubble-strewn, shrunken in its outsized bed, and a cooling wind begins to stir. As we near Panorama Point, Rainier's sister volcanoes, Mount Adams and the shattered crater of Mount Saint Helens, rise above the rugged peaks of the Tatoosh Range. Beyond us, the upper Nisqually icefall lifts to the broad blue-white shoulder of the mountain's crest. Up here it's all whiteness and sky. When we reach Panorama Point, Caitlin scrambles onto a rock and holds Hiking Bear up for a better view. The sky is cloudless and wind from the glacier unfurls her hair in red streamers in the sunlight.

The camera is in my pack, of course, but the image imprints itself indelibly. I imagine the mountain capturing yet another heart—like a midge in the sticky petals of a catchfly—as its white and icy leaves unfold blossomlike in the dazzling summer sunlight.

 Moon, owl,
subalpine firs, Paradise

31

Chapter One

IMAGE AND QUEST
THE MOUNTAIN AND THE HUMAN LANDSCAPE

Like the meltwater streams that radiate out from its icy cap, Mount Rainier casts a net of wonderment over a wide and varied geography. The mountain spills its magic over cities and freeways, farm fields and tidal flats, and over a small sea of humans that has pooled like morning clouds at its feet. The mountain remains little changed since humans first approached its slopes, but our perception of it has shifted dramatically over time—from the volatile personality ascribed to the volcano by native people to the seismic restlessness we monitor on its slopes today. Tahoma nurtured a rich narrative legacy among Native Americans who made their home in its shadow, and it fastened itself mightily on the imaginations of the Europeans who followed.

Mount Rainier's power over the human imagination is well documented. It was given eloquent voice in the diaries, journals, and published reports of early visitors. What is amazing is that despite the differing values and beliefs that separate our time from theirs, the desires that drew nineteenth-century adventurers to the mountain ring true for us today. The same taste for exploration and adventure, the excitement of discovery still whets the senses of contemporary visitors to the park. And the solace we feel while immersed in

the mountain's quiet beauty is just as fulfilling.

Sometimes, when encountering a new landscape, I try to visualize what it must have been like when Europeans first set foot in it—the Columbia Gorge of Lewis and Clark, Captain Vancouver's Puget Sound shoreline. At Mount Rainier, thanks to the vision of its earliest explorers, scientists, and conservationists, I don't have to imagine what it was once like. Within Mount Rainier National Park, the wilderness endures largely intact. Here the elements that continue to shape human culture in the Pacific Northwest—imagination and landscape—remain forever joined.

IN 1792 CAPTAIN GEORGE VANCOUVER WAS SEARCHING for the rumored Northwest Passage when he sailed his war sloop *Discovery* into the inland waters and first caught sight of the "round snowy mountain" rising above the forested shoreline. In the tradition of seafarers of his day, he noted its coordinates in his log and named it for his fellow officer in the Royal British Navy, Peter Rainier. A trickle of Europeans settled the shores beneath the snowy peak in the decades that followed, sparsely at first, then in a steady stream. Given the mountain's proximity to the coastal settlements of Puget Sound, it's not surprising that less than a

35

century passed before it attained prominence as a recreational magnet and icon for the region.

In 1870 the capital of Washington Territory was a village of two thousand souls, and a trip overland from Olympia to the slopes of Mount Rainier was itself a wilderness expedition. The two adventurers who completed the first recorded ascent of the mountain that year reported the intervening country as bristling with immense forests and nearly impassable with fallen trees, upturned roots, and "a perfect jungle of undergrowth."

After a full day's ride on their reconnaissance from the capital, Hazard Stevens and Philemon B. Van Trump emerged from the forest onto Yelm Prairie startled by their view of the mountain. It was, as Stevens later recorded, "bathed in cold, white, spectral light from summit to base." Stevens, who had received the Congressional Medal of Honor for bravery during the Civil War, confessed to a little dread mingled with his admiration. This quiet clash of emotions echoed centuries of Native American regard for the mountain and anticipated the feelings of many climbers who

Clearing storm *The power and mystique of Mount Rainier drew early Native American hunters and gatherers to its slopes long before it lured European pilgrims and adventurers. The earliest known human presence on the mountain dates back more than two thousand years.*

approach the mountain for the first time today.

Stevens grew up in the shadow of the mountain. He was the son of Isaac Stevens, the first governor of Washington Territory, and had accompanied his father on his travels to negotiate treaties with Northwest tribes. Van Trump was secretary to the presiding governor. Both were influential in current affairs of the future state. And both would figure prominently in the popularization of Mount Rainier. Van Trump, in fact, become a lifelong promoter of the glories of the mountain.

At Yelm, the party persuaded James Longmire to guide them to the base of the peak. One of the earliest homesteaders in the area, Longmire had led the first wagon train across the mountains by way of the Indian trail over Naches Pass in 1853, and he later improved an old Indian trail up the Mashel and Nisqually rivers. Eventually, he would open the first hotel in what is now the park. As much as anyone, he would be responsible for our current perception of the mountain. With a third member, Edmund T. Coleman, a mountaineer from Victoria with

experience in the Alps, the party traveled east along the Nisqually River bottom, winding around downed trees and pushing through tangled vine maple thickets. The trail was faint to nonexistent, the weather hot, and the gnats and mosquitoes relentless. They crossed tracts of open prairie, forded the icy rush of the Nisqually, and picked their way through "labyrinths of fallen timber." Several days of tough travel brought them to Bear Prairie near the present southern border of the park. There, Longmire secured the services of a Yakama Indian named Sluiskin to guide them up to the glaciers.

Hazard Stevens and **Philemon B. Van Trump** *Although Lieutenant August Kautz nearly reached the summit in 1857 and others later claimed to have made the ascent, the first recorded climb of Mount Rainier was made by Stevens* (left) *and Van Trump in August of 1870. Van Trump later became one of the strongest advocates for a national park.*

Sluiskin was a remarkable character. Living independently off the reservation and clinging to the old hunting ways, he was well versed in trading jargon and had a considerable stock of English. He was also possessed of a keen intelligence and "a shrewd sarcastic wit." When Longmire and Stevens found him, he was camped with his wife and two children, cradling a Hudson's Bay rifle while his wife cured a hide. He made a memorable impression on Stevens: ". . . a tall slender Indian clad in buckskin shirt and leggings, with a striped woolen breech-clout, and a singular head garniture which gave him a fierce and martial appearance." He sported an old military cap decorated with strips of fur and eagle feathers, its visor adorned with brass studs. Sluiskin knew the mountain well —his family had hunted its slopes extensively—and he agreed to guide them to snowline. But he dismissed out of hand their intent to climb. It was impossible. Perhaps to dissuade them from their folly, perhaps to discourage any who might be foolish enough to follow, he led the party on an exhausting, circuitous route.

Sluiskin took them directly up a steep slope to the crest of the rugged Tatoosh Range south of the mountain. Coleman soon fell behind, lost his pack, and retreated to wait at Bear Prairie. Over the next two days, their guide led them on a demanding traverse along the exposed crest of the range. At last, "creeping on hands and knees over loose rocks, and clinging to scanty tufts of grass where a single slip would have sent us rolling a thousand feet down to destruction, —we reached the highest crest." Their view of Mount Rainier and its surrounding ridges and valleys was spectacular. That afternoon they descended to Paradise Valley, rested briefly, then followed Mazama Ridge to a high camp in a grove of subalpine firs.

That night, as Stevens and Van Trump made preparations for their climb, Sluiskin realized they were serious. Now he changed tactics and pled with the two men to abandon their foolhardy plan.

Takhoma, he said, was an enchanted mountain, inhabited by an evil spirit, who dwelt in a fiery lake on its summit. No human being could ascend it or even attempt its ascent, and survive. At first, indeed, the way was easy. The broad snowfields, over which he had so often

Sluiskin Falls and the Tatoosh Range *Stevens and Van Trump's guide on the mountain was a Yakama man named Sluiskin. In an attempt to discourage them from climbing the mountain, he led them on a demanding approach over the crest of the Tatoosh Range to a camp above Sluiskin Falls.*

38

hunted the mountain goat, interposed no obstacle, but above them the real adventurer would be compelled to climb up steeps of loose, rolling rocks, which would turn beneath his feet and cast him headlong into the deep abyss below. The upper slopes, too, were so steep that not even a goat, far less a man, could get over them. And he would have to pass below lofty walls and precipices whence avalanches of snow and vast masses of rock were continually falling; and these would inevitably bury the intruder beneath their ruins. Moreover, a furious tempest continu-ally swept the crown of the mountain, and the luckless adventurer, even if he escaped the perils below, would be torn from the mountain and whirled through the air by this fearful blast. And the awful being on the summit, who would surely punish the sacrilegious attempt to invade his sanctuary,—who could hope escape his vengeance? Many years ago, he continued, his grandfather, a great chief and warrior, and a mighty hunter, had ascended part way up the mountain, and had encountered some of these dangers, but he fortunately turned back in time to escape destruction; and no other Indian has ever gone so far.

When he failed to convince them, Sluiskin settled into a funeral dirge mourning their imminent deaths. To Stevens, lying awake in his blanket, the dim glow of the mountain above him, the roar of meltwater streams below, and the thunder of avalanches only heightened the "weird effect" of Sluiskin's song.

Sluiskin's description of the climb, dramatic as it was, was remarkably accurate, suggesting that Native Americans may have been more intimate with the mountain's upper slopes than history has acknowledged. Even the "fiery lake" and "awful being" of the summit may have some basis in fact. The earliest historical eruptions of the mountain were between 1820 and 1854, well within the lifetimes of Sluiskin's father and grandfather. At any rate, Stevens knew from a heroic 1857 attempt on the mountain by Lieutenant August Kautz, that the summit could be reached.

Kautz's party had also approached by way of the Nisqually River and ascended the glacier that now bears his name. At the end of a long day of climbing, his party exhausted, Kautz pushed on alone to nearly 14,000 feet, where the slope "spread out comparatively flat." But the lateness of the day and

Sluiskin *Fearing for the lives of the important "Bostons" in his charge, Sluiskin tried to persuade Stevens and Van Trump to abandon their plan to climb the volcano. Failing in that, he demanded a "paper" holding him blameless in their all-but-certain deaths.*

The mountain, lupine, and pink heather from Pinnacle Peak *William Fraser Tolmie's 1833 "botanizing expedition" to the mountain collected a number of plants new to science.*

high freezing winds turned him back short of the summit. Northwest climber and mountaineering historian Fred Beckey called the attempt "the most enterprising American mountaineering expedition up to that time."

Historians point to two earlier attempts made on the mountain, though they were not well known at the time. In the summer of 1852, a party of four settlers led by Sidney Ford were reported to have climbed the peak while exploring a cross-Cascade wagon route. And an 1855 ascent by two unnamed surveyors was reported years later by their Indian guide. Neither party left a firsthand record of their climb, however, and Fred Beckey advises "a certain skepticism" regarding the claims.

The very first European to set foot in the area of the present park did so decades earlier. In the summer of 1833 a young Scotsman, Dr. William Fraser Tolmie, arrived at the Hudson's Bay Company's Fort Nisqually. The massive peak dominating the eastern horizon caught the botanist's imagination, and he soon received permission for a ten-day botanizing excursion to the mountain. Accompanied by Nisqually and Puyallup guides, Tolmie followed the valleys of the Puyallup and Mowich rivers into the northwest corner of the park, but the expedition was a miserable one. His first night out, camped beneath a tree in steady rain, a limb broke loose and crashed across his leg causing considerable pain. The rains were persistent. He was barely able to keep up with his guides and was often cold, wet, and hungry. Nonetheless, his diary entries reveal a startling sensitivity to and appreciation of the landscape. Tolmie ascended the Mount Pleasant–Hessong Rock ridge above Spray Park just northwest of the mountain and had a spectacular, close-up view. "Mount Rainier appeared surpassingly splendid and magnificent," he wrote, ". . . & is bounded on each side by bold bluff crags scantily covered with stunted pines." Tolmie collected a number of botanical samples from the area, and several Northwest plant species now bear his name.

Twenty years later a young travel writer named Theodore Winthrop crossed the Cascades just north and east of the mountain. His 1862 book *The Canoe and the Saddle* became a national best-seller. Winthrop's prose was effusive: "Studying the light and majesty of Tacoma, there passed from it and entered into my being, to dwell there evermore by the side of many such, a thought and an image of solemn beauty. . ." etc. But his book introduced numerous readers to the

mountain in the decade prior to Stevens and Van Trump's successful climb.

The pair were determined to reach the summit and carried the flag and brass plaque to prove it. They rose before dawn on August 17 and started up the snowfields in the first light. Carrying alpenstocks, an ice axe, and a rope, with primitive crampons they called "creepers" strapped to their boots, they made good time, reaching the prominent outcrop of Gibraltar Rock in a few hours. They crawled across the face of Gibraltar on a narrow, exposed ledge, ducking frequent rockfall, and ascended a chute of ice and rock before reaching the upper Nisqually Glacier. Winds on the upper peak were fierce and cold, forcing the climbers to brace themselves against their alpenstocks and to "use great caution to guard ourselves from being swept off the ridge." After eleven hours of

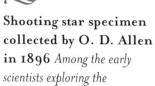

Shooting star specimen collected by O. D. Allen in 1896 *Among the early scientists exploring the mountain was Yale University botanist O. D. Allen. His sons Edward and Grenville later assumed active roles in resource management in the new national park.*

41

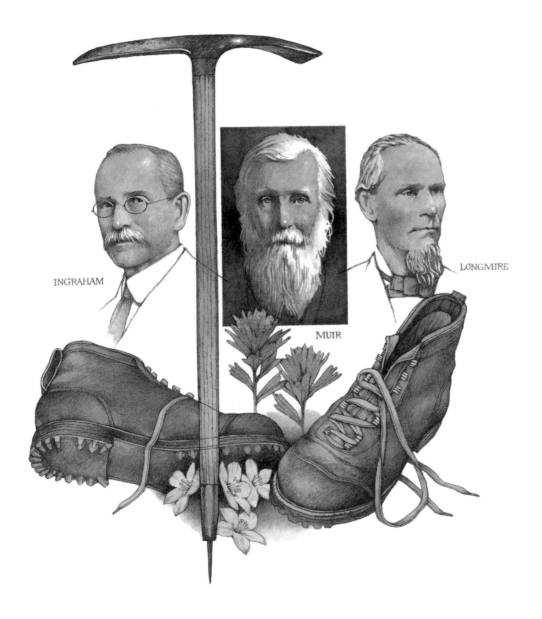

INGRAHAM

MUIR

LONGMIRE

climbing, they reached the summit. The lowlands were shrouded in smoke and mist and "the winds were now a perfect tempest, and bitterly cold." Chilled to the bone, exhausted, and afraid to descend in the coming darkness, they decided to spend the night in the steam caves they discovered in the west crater. They spent a miserable bivouac, nauseated by hydrogen sulfide and alternately freezing and being scalded by steam. The following day, when they returned to their camp, sun-burned, ragged, and spent, Sluiskin thought they were ghosts.

News of Stevens and Van Trump's successful ascent received nationwide publicity and focused widespread interest on the mountain. Within months, geologists Samuel Emmons and A. D. Wilson repeated the climb, and others followed. In 1883, Van Trump returned to the mountain with James Longmire and the well-known California mountaineer George Bayley to make his second successful summit climb. Longmire's participation in this climb would lead directly to his pivotal role in opening the mountain to popular tourism.

Rainier's reputation and popularity as a mountaineering goal grew rapidly, particularly after John Muir—accompanied by Van Trump, E. S. Ingraham, the artist William Keith, and Seattle photographer Arthur Warner—reached the summit in 1888. Muir's lyric account of the climb, published in the *Pacific Monthly,* and Warner's photographs, the first from high on the peak, evoked the majesty of the mountain for armchair travelers throughout the West. Muir called the ascent of Rainier "the grandest excursion of all to be made" in the Northwest, and his description of the subalpine parklands of Paradise was the first to capture their magic.

Here, the vast continuous woods at length begin to give way. . . leaving smooth spacious parks, with here and there separate groups of trees standing out in the midst of openings like islands in a lake. Every one of these parks, great and small, is a garden filled knee-deep with fresh, lovely flowers of every hue, the most luxurious and the most extravagantly beautiful of all the Alpine gardens I ever beheld in all my mountain-top ramblings.

Muir's party spent a chill and restless night above Paradise at a high camp that was renamed by Ingraham

in honor of its famous guest. At 4:00 A.M. the next morning they were off for the summit. The party followed the Gibraltar route pioneered by Van Trump and Stevens, stopping to drive steel caulks into their boots for the ascent of the upper glaciers. "It was nerve-trying work," Muir later recalled, "but we made good speed nevertheless, and by noon all stood

Paradise Park and the Tatoosh Range *The Salish name for these meadows is* Saghalie Illahe *or "land of peace." John Muir called them "the lower gardens of Eden." Their current name echoes those earlier sentiments.*

43

Early climbers *After the turn of the century, increasing numbers of climbers explored Rainier's upper snowfields and glaciers. Climbing fashion of the day tended toward mixed parties, long alpenstocks, and large groups.* **Helen Holmes** *(top left) reached the summit in 1894. Four years earlier, Fay Fuller, a school teacher from Yelm, became the first woman to make the climb.*

together on the utmost summit." He described the expansive view from the summit as "map-like." The mountains and forests stretched far into Oregon, the great volcanic cones of the Cascades floating like "islands in the sky." Muir noted by its craters that Rainier was a relatively young volcano, and that its summit ice cap fed all of its glaciers. His keen observations and eloquent descriptive prose were in no small part responsible for a renewed rush of attention that in little more than a decade would see the mountain and its surrounding forests preserved as a national park.

In the late nineteenth century, increasingly urbanized Americans began to turn to wilderness landscapes as refuges for the soul. America lacked the cathedrals and museums of Europe. The writings of Muir and others extolled the primeval North American landscape and evoked this spiritual element of the wilderness experience. Railroads also promoted the scenic wonders of the American West, and thousands of urban residents began to plan their recreational outings in the wildlands of the West.

𝒯T IS FITTING THAT THE THE MAN WHO GUIDED SO MANY early climbers to Mount Rainier would be the one to usher the first waves of recreational tourists to the mountain's slopes. When James Longmire accompanied his old friend Philemon Van Trump to Rainier's summit in 1883, he was sixty-three. It had been thirty years since he first settled on Yelm Prairie. He remembered his first sight of the prairie, thick with its tall waving grasses, and the mountain "standing guard over all in its snowy coat." As Longmire returned to his party's camp on the Nisqually River after his climb, he discovered his pack horses had wandered off. After a short search he found them grazing in a meadow on a bench above the river. He also found mineral springs near the meadow's edge. At the time such springs were believed to cure a host of ills, and Longmire saw the commercial potential for a spa at the site. He returned the following year to establish Longmire's Medical Springs.

Longmire and his sons built a modest log inn to house visitors. Later, with the help of a crew of Indian laborers, he cleared 13 miles of primitive trail to create a "road" to the springs. Once tied in with an existing wagon road from Yelm, Longmire's road made Mount Rainier accessible for the first time from the population centers of Puget Sound. His widespread advertising popularized not only his rustic resort but the scenic wonders of the mountain as well. By 1890 he found it necessary to construct a two-story, split-cedar hotel to handle the increasing numbers of visitors.

～ **James Longmire established Longmire's Mineral Springs** *in 1884. Early visitors traveled to the resort for its spectacular setting as much as for the questionable health benefits of its mineral baths.* **The mountain** (above) *as seen from Longmire meadow today.*

Camp of the Clouds at Paradise *Early visitors to the park's high country were likely to stay in one of the popular tent camps that offered board and lodging. John Reese established what became Camp of the Clouds in 1897. By 1914 it boasted seventy tents.*

Although Longmire's Springs was billed as a restorative health spa, many of its guests were attracted to the magnificent wild landscape that surrounded it. The Longmire family improved a trail from the springs to Paradise Park and introduced hundreds of visitors to the stunning subalpine meadowlands that blanket the southern slopes of the mountain. James's

grandson Len Longmire served as a mountain guide, leading clients to Rainier's summit for a fee of one dollar. In 1890 one early climber, a young teacher and journalist from Yelm named Fay Fuller, became the first woman to reach the summit.

Paradise Park grew in popularity, supporting a coffee shop in 1895 and a tent camp a year later. Other parts of the mountain were soon coming into their own as tourist destinations as well. Tent camps similar to those at Paradise later sprang up at Indian Henry's Hunting Ground and Ohanapecosh. In 1897 the Oregon Mazamas (a newly formed alpine club that ten years later would seed The Mountaineers in Seattle) made their first expedition to the mountain. The Longmire family led pack trains from the rail head at Yelm, and the Northern Pacific Railroad's fashionable Tacoma Hotel sponsored summer excursions to Moraine Park on the north side of the mountain. As a tourist Mecca, Mount Rainier had arrived.

Seattle and Tacoma's populations exploded with the arrival of the transcontinental railroads in the 1880s and 1890s, and urban crowds flocking to the mountain brought problems. Fragile meadows were being trampled; subalpine trees were cut down for tent poles and firewood (entire groves were set ablaze for the delight of tourists); game animals were becoming scarce due to overhunting. Commercial interests were also threatening the mountain's pristine beauty. Visitors encountered wide expanses of clearcut and burned-over forests in the lower valleys approaching the mountain, and grazing by sheep (Muir's "hoofed locusts") was beginning to occur on the mountain's high meadows. Miners had discovered the mountain as well; by 1898, forty-one claims were filed in Glacier Basin alone. Pressure to protect the region's premiere scenic area began to mount.

THE DRIVE TO PRESERVE MOUNT RAINIER FROM destruction and commercial exploitation was part of a newly emerging nationwide campaign to save wildlands throughout the West. This movement's foremost spokesman was John Muir. A popular and outspoken defender of wilderness, Muir wrote eloquently of the need to protect forest and mountain

wilderness as national parks. In the American transcendentalist tradition of Emerson and Thoreau, Muir saw in wild nature the earthly manifestations of the Creator. "The clearest way into the Universe," he wrote, "is through a forest wilderness."

Yellowstone, the nation's first national park was created in 1872. Yosemite, Sequoia, and General Grant (later King's Canyon) followed in 1890. The next year, responding to popular pressure to protect the nation's forestlands from destructive logging practices, Congress granted the president authority to establish forest reserves. In 1893 President Harrison established the Pacific Forest Reserve, which surrounded Mount Rainier, by presidential proclamation. Establishment of the reserve did little to protect the scenic resources of Mount Rainier, however; mining, grazing, and unrestricted recreational use continued. A short while later a presidential committee on the management of forest reserves—to which Muir served as advisor— recommended that Mount Rainier and Grand Canyon be preserved as national parks. Muir carried the theme

Visitors on the road to Paradise *In the park's early years auto traffic stopped at the Nisqually River crossing, a stone's throw from the terminus of the Nisqually Glacier. Travelers made the rest of the trip on horseback or by carriage.* **Nisqually Glacier** (far right) *continued to recede throughout the twentieth century to its present terminus nearly a mile up valley.*

of protection for the mountain to a national audience. "Of all the fire mountains which, like beacons, once blazed along the Pacific Coast," he wrote in the *Atlantic Monthly,* "Mount Rainier is the noblest in form, has the most interesting forest cover, and . . . is the highest and most flowery." He urged that it "should be made a national park and guarded while yet its bloom is on."

Throughout the campaign for a park, it was those who had experienced the mountain most intimately, by climbing it and exploring its slopes, who became its most passionate advocates. As early as 1883 a British writer and a German geologist recognized the mountain's world-class qualities and wrote Congress recommending the area be protected as a national park. In 1891 Van Trump picked up the idea and worked tirelessly for the creation of a park. Local newspapers and mountain clubs soon joined the cause. A number of prominent scientists and university faculty who had visited the mountain helped popularize the park idea through articles and lectures. In 1894 the National Geographic Society, the

Geological Society of America, and the American Association for the Advancement of Science, along with the Sierra Club and the Appalachian Mountain Club formally petitioned Congress to establish a national park for Mount Rainier. But the growing campaign for a park may have received its most powerful boost from an unlikely source.

The Northern Pacific Railroad, which in 1864 had received a generous federal land grant of alternating one-mile sections throughout much of the West, had a keen interest in Rainier's designation as a national park. Already the railroad was shuttling tourists to the Carbon River valley, but there were other motives as well. The park bill, as drafted by a congressman friendly to railroad interests, allowed Northern Pacific to exchange sections of economically worthless rock and ice in what are now the Mount Baker–Snoqualmie and Gifford Pinchot national forests, acre for acre, for some of the most valuable forest and mineral lands in the Northwest. As part of Mount Rainier's legacy, thousands of acres of publicly owned forestlands passed from the public domain to

The National Park Inn
opened for business at Longmire in 1906. Built by the Tacoma Eastern Railroad, it boasted a French chef and chamber music by the fire in the social hall. It far outclassed rustic Longmire's Springs across the road, but eleven years later it too was trumped by the elegant Paradise Inn.

the Northern Pacific Company and on to private timber interests.

These currents converged in the final years of the nineteenth century, and after several false starts, a bill to create Mount Rainier National Park "for the benefit and enjoyment of the people" was passed by Congress and signed into law by President McKinley on March 2, 1899. The Northwest finally had its first national park. Somewhat weakened by compromise, the act left out some 300 square miles of valuable lowland forest that had been included in the park bill as originally proposed by conservationists and allowed mining to continue in the new park. Both problems would be addressed in future legislation.

For several years the new park was an orphan, without a budget appropriation or a full-time superintendent, but that did not slow the stream of visitors. About two thousand people journeyed to the park during its first year of existence; within fifteen years visitation approached thirty-five thousand. Early tourists continued to concentrate at Longmire and Paradise. James Longmire died two years before the

park was established, but the Longmire family maintained its rustic hotel and mineral springs. In 1906 the Tacoma Eastern Railroad Company constructed the National Park Inn. It was located opposite Longmire Springs but catered to a different clientele. The modern hotel housed sixty guests and served meals prepared by a French chef. After dinner guests were entertained by musicians before the fireplace in the social hall. The following year, guests began to arrive at the inn in autos—a harbinger of the hordes of motorized tourists to come. Though the park experience was beginning to change, most visitors were still packed in on horseback and stayed in tent camps. Camp of the Clouds at Paradise grew from seven tents and a cook tent in 1903 to a village of seventy tents by 1914. The rates with board were modest, $2.50 per person per day or $14 per week, and the fare was plain but reportedly ample. By 1908 Indian Henry's Hunting Ground supported a similar, but smaller, tent camp called the Wigwam Hotel.

In the early years of the park most visitors to Mount Rainier lacked the equipment to camp on their

own. Those who could were likely to belong to one of the region's new mountaineering clubs. The climbing fashion of the day tended toward large organized expeditions, and the summer of 1905 saw two sizable climbing encampments at Paradise. The Sierra Club of San Francisco sponsored a large Mount Rainier outing that year, and the Mazamas of Portland mounted an expedition of more than two hundred. For two weeks in August the camps were the scenes of great social gatherings. The trail between the camps "saw many a fantastic procession of mountaineers winding its way by moonlight among the giant fir trees." The socializing culminated near the end of the outings in a mock wedding of the two clubs, the bride trailing a long flowing veil of mosquito netting.

The clubs, forerunners of today's national environmental organizations, fostered a conservation ethic among their members, encouraging an appreciation of the mountain environment through understanding. Scientists and educators among the parties were called upon to give campfire talks as a regular part of club outings. The tradition of evening interpretive programs by park naturalists at Rainier may have had its first expression among these early gatherings.

Something else was undoubtedly taking root during those 1905 expeditions that would play an important role in the future development of the new park. A year after the climb, Seattle members of the Mazamas split off to form their own outdoor club, The Mountaineers, thus beginning a long and intimate involvement with the park that continues today. In 1909 noted outdoor photographer Asahel Curtis led The Mountaineers' third annual outing to Moraine Park. A large party of enthusiastic climbers reached the summit by way of the Winthrop and Emmons glaciers. Six years later more than one hundred Mountaineers returned to the park for a hiking trip around the mountain on the not-yet-completed Wonderland Trail; about half the group also climbed to the summit. After "three glorious weeks above the clouds," the party returned to Tacoma and Seattle by "prosaic old railroad." But their experiences on the mountain generated much-needed support for sound management in the new park. An organized effort by The Mountaineers led to the appointment of a full-time superintendent in 1910, as well as the establishment of standards for licensed guides on the mountain. The club also successfully lobbied Congress to increase appropriations for the park and to expand its boundaries.

By 1915 as many as thirty-five thousand people were visiting Mount Rainier annually and existing accommodations and resources were strained. That year Stephen T. Mather, a Chicago area businessman and veteran of the 1905 Sierra Club outing who was soon to become director of the newly established National Park Service, returned to the park in the company of Asahel Curtis. Curtis, best known now for his remarkable outdoor photography, was a key player in the formative years of the park. At the time he effectively straddled two worlds. A founding member of The Mountaineers, he was an avid promoter and talented chronicler of the wilderness experience. He was also a tenacious booster of commercial development in the park. After their trip along the rugged west side of the park, Curtis arranged a

meeting between Mather and a group of prominent Seattle and Tacoma businessmen at the Rainier Club. Mather offered the group an exclusive concession for recreational developments in the park and easily convinced them to form a partnership. The Rainier National Park Company was soon established. The following year the company bought out the independent tent camp operations and construction was begun on a grand hotel for Paradise. The luxurious Paradise Inn

Members of the 1915 Mountaineers outing on the summit *The Mountaineers spent three weeks circling the mountain on the not-yet-complete Wonderland Trail that year. On August 14, more than fifty climbers reached the summit by way of Camp Curtis and the Emmons Glacier.*

Stephen T. Mather (top)
and Eugene Ricksecker

opened in July 1917. The inn's cathedral-like lobby was framed with silvery Alaska yellow-cedar logs; its spacious dining room comfortably sat four hundred guests. The hotel in its spectacular setting attracted visitors from across the country, and a one hundred-room annex was soon added. Mount Rainier was now a national tourist destination.

When Stephen Mather took over the newly created National Park Service, he was given a demanding assignment. The 1916 Organic Act charged his agency to "conserve the scenery and the natural and historic objects and the wildlife therein and to provide for the enjoyment of same and in such manner and such means as will leave them unimpaired for the enjoyment of future generations." Preservationists like John Muir saw in this directive a firm emphasis on conserving park resources to leave them unimpaired for future generations. Director Mather, however, felt a pressing need to develop the parks in ways that would attract increasing numbers of newly mobilized visitors and insure popular support for his fledgling agency

and for the national park idea. Among the national parks at the time, Mount Rainier had the unique advantage of lying in close proximity to a burgeoning urban population and enjoying overwhelming local support. Mather took a personal interest in its development.

In the early years of the park, a civilian engineer from the War Department named Eugene Ricksecker was assigned the task of surveying and constructing an improved road from the Nisqually entrance to Paradise. Ricksecker envisioned a "pleasure road," designed to conform with mountain topography. He laid out a scenic byway that would keep the traveler "in a keen state of expectancy as to the new pleasures held in store at the next turn." Ricksecker's road was opened in 1915, and with a few modifications it remains one of the more enjoyable scenic drives in the Northwest today.

By 1920 most of the remainder of the park was still roadless. But Mather, at the prompting of Asahel Curtis and his Seattle-Tacoma business associates, was initiating plans for roaded access to each corner of the park. Within a decade all of the roads in the park today—Carbon River, White River, Sunrise, Stevens Canyon, the West Side Road—were either completed, under construction, or surveyed. Plans were even laid for a one-way scenic drive to Alta Vista and Panorama Point above Paradise! It was around this time that con-servationists stepped in to voice their concern.

In 1921 Irving Clark of The Mountaineers helped persuade Pierce County and Forest Service officials to complete the connecting link for the Carbon River Road in the park. But by 1928 The Mountaineers lodged a formal protest to the Park Service. The club charged that the Park Service's current frenzy of road construction was excessive and "would subject approximately three-fourths of the park to commercial use and development." The Mountaineers then introduced a visionary idea. They proposed that a portion of the park be declared a wilderness area, accessible only by foot and pack stock. Park managers took notice, and that same year the entire northern portion of the park and a section of the west side of the mountain were placed in a

The mountain from Ricksecker Point (above) and **Narada Falls** *The road to Paradise was designed to incorporate striking vistas along its route and give travelers an intimate sense of the landscape. The original road crossed the river at Narada Falls. Today Ricksecker's road remains one of the most scenic in the Northwest.*

designation that prohibited roads and development. They remain a wilderness today.

Historians have pointed out that management of the national parks over the past century reflects our

55

Mass transit circa 1920
Several inns and concessions transported guests in "stages" from rail heads outside the park. As current auto congestion worsens on park roads during the summer season, managers are rethinking the role of shuttle buses in the park.

changing values and levels of scientific understanding. Early parks like Yellowstone and Mount Rainier were established largely to protect scenery from commercial exploitation. The act creating Mount Rainier mandates that "regulations shall provide for the preservation from injury or spoliation of all timber, mineral deposits, natural curiosities or wonders." It was only with increased ecological awareness that Americans came to see the parks as preserves where natural processes should be allowed to continue with minimum human interference. Few early parks were established with boundaries adequate "to conserve the natural and historic objects and the wildlife therein" as mandated by the 1916 Organic Act, and Mount Rainier was no exception.

A utilitarian ethic, as promoted by Gifford Pinchot's Forest Service, prevailed throughout the natural sciences of the day. As a result, limited grazing, mining, and hunting were allowed in the parks. Forests were valued for their green, healthy, and productive trees. Dead and dying trees and downed logs—now recognized as invaluable habitat components of

old-growth forests—were seen as unhealthy blights on the landscape. Mount Rainier National Park was barely a decade old before a salvage logging sale was let on dead trees along the lower Nisqually road. In 1910 a much larger redcedar salvage sale, which threatened to take live as well as dead trees, was vigorously opposed by conservationists and subsequently halted. Later, a wartime effort by the state of Washington to allow fifty thousand sheep to graze in the park's subalpine meadows was also turned back by popular opposition. A memorable highlight of that early campaign came when members of The Mountaineers volunteered to pasture sheep on their front lawns to support the war effort rather than open the park to commercial grazing. But even the conservation community, largely made up of sportsmen, failed to object to the Park Service's wildlife policy of reducing the numbers of "undesirable" wildlife species (i.e., predators: wolf, cougar, bobcat, lynx) to increase "desirable" wildlife (i.e., game animals: deer, elk, mountain goat, bear). In the 1910s and 1920s park rangers and, occasionally, hired trappers hunted predators at Mount Rainier during the winter months. It was during this time that wolves disappeared from the area around the park and wolverines, river otters, and fishers became scarce. Not until 1930, when a national directive prohibited the killing of predators in parks, did the strategy of "natural regulation"—maintaining a healthy balance of predators and prey—become Park Service policy.

In the meantime Mount Rainier's popularity continued to increase; the number of visitors to the park reached a record quarter million in 1929. With the onset of the Depression, however, many families were unable to afford even weekend trips to the park. Visitation fell by nearly half in the early 1930s. Business at the Paradise Inn and the newly opened Sunrise Lodge in Yakima Park foundered. Restaurants stood mostly empty, but picnic areas were full and campgrounds became suddenly popular. More than ever before, economy-minded visitors eschewed concessionaire-guided horseback trips and struck out on park trails afoot. While most hikers stuck close to developed areas around Paradise and Sunrise, newly constructed backcountry shelters lured the more

adventurous into the roadless wilds of the park.

In an effort to attract more guests to its flagging hotels, the Rainier National Park Company embarked on the most flagrant round of overdevelopment to be visited upon the park's high meadows in its history. A nine-hole golf course was constructed at Paradise.

Dogsled touring at Paradise *Among the contrivances cooked up to attract visitors to flagging park inns was a short-lived dogsled concession.*

58

climb at Paradise. On the east side of the mountain a wild West theme prevailed; Sunrise Lodge was billed as "Sunrise Dude Ranch," complete with cowboys, Indians, and a mythical landscape of cattle range, gold mines and a hideout used by cattle rustlers.

One area where tourist promotions paid off handsomely was in winter use. The newly discovered sport of downhill skiing arrived at Paradise in 1934 in the form of the first annual Silver Skis race, a steep run from Camp Muir to Paradise. The following year the National Ski Association brought its championship downhill and slalom races to the mountain. The event was attended by 7,500 spectators and broadcast around the country. Downhill skiing became immensely popular; a European instructor was imported, and Mount Rainier became the premiere ski resort in the Northwest. Within a few years a rope tow appeared at Paradise. Not long after, developers and ski clubs mounted a twenty-year campaign to construct a modern chairlift to Panorama Point. The proposal was finally put to rest by the Park Service in 1954 when conservationists opposing the

("Golf is a country game," announced Mather's successor Horace Albright, "It can be justified in parks easier than tennis.") A boat house and rental concession sprouted on the pristine shores of Reflection Lake. A motorcycle club even staged a hill

tram outnumbered supporters by ten to one.

The Depression years opened another unique chapter in the park's history, the era of the Civilian Conservation Corps (CCC) and other New Deal public works projects. The Park Service joined Roosevelt's effort to put America to work, and by the mid-1930s nearly a thousand young men from around the country were employed in six summer work camps in the park. All were between eighteen and twenty-five and all were from families on relief. CCC crews became legendary in the national parks, accomplishing incredible amounts of conservation and resource work under close professional guidance. At Rainier, crews refurbished the trails, picnic areas, and campgrounds so much in demand by economy-minded visitors of the 1930s. They revegetated road cuts and stabilized erosive slopes, built picnic shelters, comfort stations, and interpretive overlooks, maintained phone and power lines, and constructed backcountry bridges and shelters. Impressive stonework shelters built by CCC crews still stand at Summerland and Indian Bar. In fact it's difficult to wander very far anywhere in the

park today without encountering their handiwork. Their era marks a high point in our society's shared commitment to social reform and natural resource protection.

World War II put an end to New Deal public works programs in the parks as young men left CCC camps for military boot camps. Families stayed home as well during the war years, and park visitation

Puget Sound and the Olympics from Mother Mountain *Unique among national parks in the early twentieth century, Mount Rainier drew most of its visitors from the nearby cities of Puget Sound. The same pattern of predominantly local use holds true today.*

dropped by nearly three-quarters. One noted exception was the winter training of ski troops from the Tenth Mountain Division stationed at Fort Lewis. Conditions on Mount Rainier simulated the harsh weather and terrain troops were expected to encounter in the European mountains in winter. Survival techniques and equipment were put to the test on the mountain's slopes, glaciers, and summit. Skills developed on Rainier and in the Colorado Rockies later proved critical to Allied operations in the mountains of Italy and the Aleutian Islands.

With advances in equipment brought by the war effort, and the general prosperity that followed, the sport of mountaineering came into its own at Mount Rainier. Professional guiding had come a long way from Len Longmire's dollar climbs in the late 1800s. Standards had been set for commercial guiding in the park early in its history, and in 1916 the Rainier National Park Company established its first commercial guide service. Interest in recreational climbing grew in the decades following the First World War, and hundreds of guided climbers reached the summit by the Gibraltar route first pioneered by Stevens and Van Trump. In the 1930s a few of The Mountaineers' more adventurous climbers like Wolf Bauer and Ome Daiber began exploring difficult routes on the north and west sides of the mountain. Parties completed impressive first ascents of Ptarmigan

~**Camping out at Paradise** *Early automobile camping in the park was a rather haphazard affair. Cars and tents sprawled over the meadows at Paradise with little consideration for subalpine vegetation.* **The proud recipients** (top) *of the park's first camping permit for Paradise.*

Ridge and Liberty Ridge in 1935. That same year Bauer and others initiated The Mountaineers' popular climbing course, which introduced thousands of Puget Sound residents to the sport. The following year Ome Daiber was called upon to assist with a well-publicized body recovery following the first winter ascent. As the sport increased in popularity, the mountain was taking its toll in climbing fatalities. Fourteen had lost their lives on the mountain thus far; over the next sixty years the number would reach seventy. Following the 1936 tragedy, Daiber, several of his fellow Mountaineers, and members of the Ski Patrol organized the first volunteer Mountain Rescue Council. It became the national model.

While a handful of experienced mountaineers were exploring new routes on Rainier, guided and independent climbing parties stuck to the familiar south side of the mountain, basing their climbs out of Paradise. In 1936 the narrow ledge across Gibraltar Rock, first "crawled" by Stevens and Van Trump, avalanched off, and guided parties turned to the Kautz Glacier route. Fifteen years later, in the early 1950s, a

pair of energetic young twins from Seattle, Jim and Lou Whittaker, took over the climbing concession in the park and reopened the Gibraltar route for guided climbs. With Camp Muir once more in use as a base camp, the popularity of climbing at Rainier grew. The number of climbers attempting the summit rose from three hundred per year in the late 1940s to five hundred in the mid-1950s. During this time Mount

Beginning in the 1930s, *the rugged north side of the mountain, cut by the Willis Wall and flanked by steep ridges, was the site of ambitious new routes. Ascents of Ptarmigan Ridge and Liberty Ridge in 1935 brought a new level of mountaineering to the Northwest.*

61

Rainier was chosen as the site of the first mountain-rescue training school for rangers from other parks and agencies. The mountain also served as a training ground for many American mountaineering expeditions to Alaska, the Yukon, and abroad. As Northwest climbers honed their technical skills in the 1950s, difficult ice routes were climbed on the steep north side of the mountain. And in 1961 the "unclimbable" Willis Wall was scaled. The names of the climbers making these and other difficult assents on the mountain—Fred Beckey, Don Claunch, Dee Molenaar, Gene Prater, Tom Hornbein, Pete Schoening, Jim Wickwire—compose a checklist of icons of Northwest mountaineering.

In 1962 mountaineering on Mount Rainier received a heroic boost when members of the well-publicized American Mount Everest Expedition trained on the mountain—in suitably severe weather. The following year Jim Whittaker became the first American to stand on the summit of the world's highest peak. He was followed by four others who had guided or climbed on Rainier. The mountain's role in the ascent of Everest did not go unnoticed by America's sport climbing community. By the mid-1960s three thousand climbers a year were kicking steps up Rainier's snowfields and glaciers. In 1968 Lou Whittaker and a partner formed Rainier Mountaineering Inc., continuing the long tradition of professionally guided summit climbs on the mountain. Today it is the oldest continually operating guide service and climbing school in the United States.

Interest in climbing and wilderness backpacking exploded with the awakening environmental consciousness of the 1970s, bringing a renewed wave of backcountry users to parks and wilderness areas throughout the States. By 1978 hikers and climbers were logging more than thirty-five thousand nights out on the mountain's slopes. While overnight use fell off some during the 1980s, a new generation of mountain adventurers has stepped in to fill the gap. The number of visitor nights out on the mountain rebounded during the 1990s and it continues to grow. Some ten thousand climbers try Rainier's icy slopes each year now, and many more backpack into the park's wild corners to steep themselves in the solitude of its ridgetops, meadows, and lakes.

In the meantime a related interest in the overall quality of life has attracted an ever-increasing population to the Pacific Northwest. The mountain that captured the imaginations of Stevens and Van Trump more than a century ago, now casts its spell over one of the fastest growing urban areas in the country. Urban recreationists stream along the route of Longmire's mountain trail at a pace that would make the old entrepreneur's head spin.

A trip to Mount Rainier National Park from the Puget Sound area now takes hours rather than days, and more than two million visitors come to experience the beauty and mystery of the mountain each year. They travel from the East Coast, from Canada, from Germany and Japan, but nearly half still come from the cities and towns within the mountain's realm. The young backpackers and climbers of the 1970s return to camp and day hike with their families, some maintaining a tradition going back generations. But the ways we enjoy the park have changed considerably from those

The Kautz Creek Mudflow *Geological activity is a constant at Mount Rainier. A volcanic mudflow or "lahar" swept down Kautz Creek in 1947. Triggered by heavy rainfall, it buried the Longmire road beneath 30 feet of debris. More recently floods and debris flows closed part of the West Side Road.*

of its earliest visitors. No longer do we come in large organized parties (though some tour bus groups to Paradise suggest something of that earlier fashion), nor do we stay for two or three weeks. Our compulsive

Trees in lifting fog, Cayuse Pass *The mountain that once caught the imaginations of Tolmie, Kautz, Stevens, and Van Trump now casts its spell over one of the fastest growing urban areas in the country. More than two million visitors drive through park entrance stations each year.*

mobility and scattered recreational priorities have shrunk the typical visit to Mount Rainier to less than a day.

Since 1915 when the first tourist-driven autos arrived sputtering and steaming at Paradise, driving to admire the park's matchless scenery has ranked as visitors' most popular activity. But more than half of those who travel to the mountain today—over a million visitors a year—leave their cars behind and take to one of the park's many trails for a day hike. Like their counterparts of a century ago, most choose Paradise.

On a warm afternoon in early autumn, I took a short stroll on a trail out of Paradise to see who the park's current visitors are. Most of the wildflowers had already gone to seed, and the huckleberry leaves were tinged with red. As might be expected, backpacks and ice axes were in short supply on the mountain that day, but the trails were alive with afternoon hikers. Kids and their parents were taking advantage of the balmy days of Indian summer for a last trip to the mountain and retired couples were eluding the summer crowds.

A tour group from Japan posed for a group photo, the cloud-capped peak rising behind them like a large and unkempt Fuji.

Above Sluiskin Falls, two boys in Mariners' caps stopped to chat while I jotted some notes near the Stevens and Van Trump memorial. They were brothers from Tacoma, they told me, and they'd left their dad panting at a rest spot. They asked what I was writing, so I told them I was interested in the different ways people have enjoyed the mountain over the last one hundred years. Soon I was embarked upon an abridged version of Rainier's first ascent. Not surprisingly, the brothers found the early mountaineers' hardships delightful, especially Sluiskin's wild goose chase over the Tatoosh Range, which loomed formidably in the distance. By the time dad caught up, Sluiskin was admonishing the climbers with his dire predictions of death and destruction. That an evil being lived in a lake of fire on the summit was way-cool to the boys, though I noticed the younger one glance nervously toward the clouded summit. A few minutes later, as I described the bedraggled climbers limping back down the trail just above us, both boys turned as if half expecting to see them. They were in agreement, too, over who they thought was the hero of the story. "Sluiskin was almost right," the younger one insisted, "They almost did die." His brother added that the icy winds could very well have blown them off the mountain, just as Sluiskin had predicted. When I mentioned my own completely safe trips to the summit, they eyed me suspiciously, as if I was as goofy as those old pioneers.

For the brothers, a late-season race to the edge of the glaciers they could glimpse from their school bus was adventure enough. From the looks of their dad slumped on a rock, it was more than enough. The boys shared a candy bar with me; their dad thanked me for the story. Then they disappeared down the trail as quickly as they had come.

The mountain, it occurred to me, is larger than our stories can measure. It enters our daily lives insistent in its presence and allure. A view from a school bus window, an afternoon hike with the kids, or a night huddled by a steam vent in the summit crater—

~ **The magnificent ancient forests** *of Mount Rainier were as much of an attraction for visitors in the early decades of the park as they are now. One of the first conservation battles within the new park was over "salvage logging" in old-growth forests.*

the magnetic pull of the mountain exceeds our imaginings. It is at once a distant dreamscape, a persistent challenge, an island of wildness in a landscape tamed to our designs.

The most recent affirmation of the central place the mountain holds in our imagination was the 1988 act of Congress that designated 97 percent of the park as a federally protected wilderness—an area, in the words of the Wilderness Act, "where the earth and its community of life are untrammeled by man, where man himself is a visitor who does not remain." It was both a confirmation and fulfillment of the act of Congress that created Mount Rainier National Park nearly a century earlier.

As the afternoon lengthened, the summit clouds lifted. I looked up at the route followed by Stevens and Van Trump, Longmire and Muir, and the thousands of adventurers who went after them. Fresh snows whitened the upper glaciers and dusted the rocky spurs. Before long winter would wrap the mountain, erasing all trace of this summer's pilgrims, and seal it behind a curtain of cloud. On those rare winter days when the mountain dawns clear and stunningly new, it will reach out to dazzle a fresh crop of sodden pilgrims. And in summer we will stream back to its slopes as faithfully as its snow-fed rivers slide past us to callings of their own.

Mountain wildflowers, Paradise Valley *The wildflower gardens of Paradise lure hundreds of thousands of visitors from their cars each year to stroll among the blooms. As our numbers continue to increase, it falls on each of us to take responsibility for protecting the natural diversity others have worked so hard to preserve.*

Chapter Two

SHARDS OF FIRE, SHEATHS OF ICE
EVOLUTION OF A VOLCANIC LANDSCAPE

The sun lifts past the mountain's shoulder as I reach the upper slopes of the glacier and floods the world with whiteness. For hours I've been working my way up the glacier in darkness, cutting wide swaths around open crevasses, pacing my breathing to crampon kicks and bites of my ice axe in the frozen snow. The slow rhythmic pace is almost hypnotic. I loosen my hood, snugged tight against the wind, and look up to see the slope mercifully beginning to ease. The vision buoys my spirit and recharges aching muscles. Before long I'm standing with my partner atop Columbia Crest, the summit of the Northwest's highest peak.

Close as we are, we're forced to shout above the wind, and the sharp cold bites through our clothes. But the dawn clouds have blown clear and the view is magnificent. From this high up, the mountainous world of the Pacific Northwest all but flattens out. The Olympics ripple off in low waves to the west, and forested uplands fall away to the east in a dim colorless plain. Even the snow-capped summits of the North Cascades seem small, distant and unimpressive. But all along the range, from Canada south into Oregon, the

ice-clad volcanoes rear over the lesser peaks, white and solitary in morning sunlight.

We can make out Garibaldi, Mount Baker, and Glacier Peak to the north, Adams, Hood, and Jefferson to the south. And close by, just to the west of Adams' bulky dome, sits the blasted shell of Mount Saint Helens. More than a mile below us and nearly 30 miles away, it is still impressive. The snow along its yawning crater is blackened with recent ashfall, and its denuded slopes are stark and gray. Since its eruption in May of 1980, Saint Helens is an ever-present reminder of the tremendous explosive potential of these magnificent snow peaks. But from my perch on Mount Rainier's summit, I don't have to look to Saint Helens for evidence that the Cascade volcanoes are alive and well. Beneath my boots the bare snow-free slopes of the crater walls and the acrid sulfurous steam that wafts up when the wind shifts leave little room for doubt. This most impressive of Cascade volcanoes shares the same fiery heritage as its self-destructive sister to the south, and its eruptive potential is every bit as real.

Governors Ridge and Tamanos Mountain
frame a distant view of Mount Adams. All of the Cascade volcanoes are part of the "Ring of Fire," a network of active volcanoes that encircles the Pacific Ocean. Fueled by the interaction of ocean and continental plates, it bristles with more than five hundred active volcanoes.

Mount Rainier, Mount Saint Helens, and all the Cascade volcanoes are part of a dynamic system of active fire mountains that encircle the Pacific in a necklace of flame. The Ring of Fire, as it is known, claims over five hundred active volcanoes, three-fourths of the world's total, and includes some of the best known and most notorious: Nevado del Ruiz in Colombia, Popocatépetl in Mexico, Katmai in Alaska, Fuji in Japan, Krakatau in Indonesia. It is no accident that so many active volcanoes occur along the margins of the Pacific Ocean, and there is little mystery about what fuels them.

Out to the west the Pacific is shrouded in a light blue haze, but beneath the calm mantle of its summer sea the ocean floor is as restless as a winter storm. The Pacific Ocean floor is spreading. It is pushing against its surrounding continents and island arcs, like a slow-turning conveyor belt, and shoving its mass beneath their edges like ore fed to a smelter. Ocean floors originate along spreading ridges where magma from deep in the earth's mantle rises up through rifts, then cools and solidifies into plates of basalt. These plates float on a deeper sea of heated semiplastic mantle and move away from their spreading ridges, carried by convection currents in the mantle beneath. When spreading seafloors run up against the edges of continents, they generally sink beneath the lighter, granitic continental plates in a process called subduction.

About 250 miles out beneath the pale blue of the Pacific, the small Juan de Fuca plate is separating from the Pacific plate along a spreading ridge. Not far off the coast of British Columbia, Washington, and Oregon, it is subducting beneath the westward drifting North American plate at a rate of an inch or two a year. As the ocean plate sinks it drags seawater-saturated sediments from the continent with it. As this concoction melts at extreme high temperatures deep within the mantle, explosive gas- and steam-charged magma works its way up through cracks and faults in the continent's edge. Often rising magma displaces rock layers a few miles beneath the surface and builds into reservoirs called magma chambers. Sometimes the magma cools in place; other times it erupts to the surface to form a volcano.

**Mount Rainier
is only the most recent
volcano** *to occupy this part
of the Cascades. At least four
waves of volcanism shook the
area over the past forty million
years. Evidence of earlier
volcanic activity, such as the
Eocene volcanic rocks of
Gobblers Knob in the
foreground, can be found
throughout the park.*

*V*OLCANISM ALONG THIS PART OF THE PACIFIC COAST IS an old story; Mount Rainier and her sister volcanoes are only the most recent installment. At one time the area that is now the Cascades in western Washington was a lowland plain of tropical swamps and sluggish river deltas accruing a sleepy blanket of sandstones and shales miles in depth. The landscape woke abruptly about forty million years ago as volcanoes erupted over the coastal plain; they then became islands as the region sank beneath a rising sea. Other mountains swelled after that, the result of tectonic buckling in the continental plate. They reached respectable heights of several thousand feet before eroding beneath millennia of rains into quiet hills.

About thirty million years ago volcanoes once more blazed across the landscape, burying the low hills beneath thick layers of pumice and smoothing the rumpled topography to a flat plain. Pumice forms when lava explodes into the air and solidifies with gas bubbles trapped in the rock. Molten lava flows more sedately, usually from broad low volcanoes like those typical of Hawaii today. These appeared next and they

inundated the area in lavas a half mile deep. More mountains rose then, faulting and shuffling the older layers of rock, rearranging rivers and forcing later geologists to work for their keep.

Then around twelve million years ago a large mass of molten rock pushed up through the older layers. Part of it erupted in a brief series of volcanoes, but most solidified beneath the surface into a pluton of handsome black and white flecked rock called granodiorite. This granite-like rock underlies nearly all of Mount Rainier from the Carbon River to the Tatoosh Range. The land rose once more a few million years ago, this time to form the familiar Cascades. Just as they do today these mountains trapped an abundance of precipitation, and rivers and glaciers eroded them into deep valleys, ridges, and peaks. By the time Mount Rainier made its first appearance, the landscape around the mountain, including the major river valleys, looked essentially as it does now.

The Mount Rainier volcano was born a brief half million years ago. Rainier's first youthful eruptions showered fountains of hot pumice into

Box Canyon, Muddy Fork of the Cowlitz River *Glacier-fed streams have carved through relatively soft volcanic rocks throughout the park. Box Canyon drops 180 feet to the opaque icemelt surge of the Muddy Fork.*

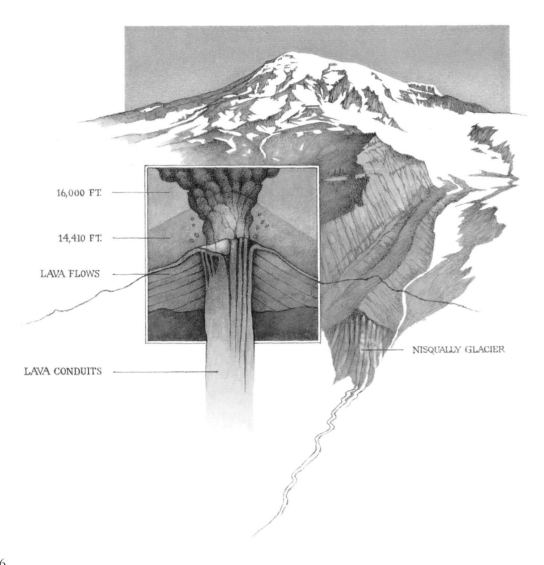

16,000 FT.

14,410 FT.

LAVA FLOWS

LAVA CONDUITS

NISQUALLY GLACIER

ash-darkened skies. It built quickly, sending thick flows of andesitic lava surging 15 miles down surrounding river valleys, filling some to depths of more than 2,000 feet. This occurred during a period of ice-age glaciation when thousands of feet of ice occupied the river valleys. Lavas flowed along the edges of these glaciers and cooled quickly against their walls. When the valley glaciers receded and meltwater rivers continued to erode their courses, the lavas remained as high isolated ridges. Today they radiate out like tree roots from the base of the peak— Rampart and Klapatche ridges, Burroughs Mountain, Grand and Yakima parks—as if anchoring the young volcano to its older mountainous terrain.

For long periods the volcano was quiet, and glaciers carved deep bowl-shaped cirques and troughs into its flanks. These quiescent times were punctuated by periods of explosive activity. Hot ash and cinders blanketed ice-covered landscapes and lava flows engulfed ice sheets, sending mudflows thundering down valleys. Lavas overrode glacial rubble, as is evidenced in many parts of the park today, and consumed meltwater

The mountain and subalpine meadows, Indian Henry's Hunting Ground

A stratovolcano, Mount Rainier was built from layers of lava, pumice, and ash. As it grew it was attacked by the erosive power of alpine glaciers. Over the last twenty-five thousand years, glaciers have carved the deeply broken topography we recognize today.

The Tahoma, Emmons, Nisqually, and Carbon glaciers (left to right)

debris. Many of Rainier's lava flows have been dated to between 100,000 and 130,000 years ago suggesting a period of vigorous volcanic activity. The mountain spewed lava flows alternately with layers of pumice and lava-cemented rubble called breccia. Continued eruptions built a massive conical layer cake, a classic strato-volcano of grand proportions.

Mount Rainier remained active through the late Pleistocene, but during the last 25,000 years climate clearly had the upper hand. Temperatures plunged; a continental ice sheet sprawled southward from Canada; winter snows deepened on the mountain, and alpine glaciers ground mercilessly into its flanks. Glaciers can be snuffed by volcanic eruptions almost

instantaneously, as was made painfully clear on Mount Saint Helens, but during times of volcanic quiescence they are agents of enormous erosive power. Glaciers thoroughly transformed the landscape of the Pacific Northwest; during the most recent Pleistocene glaciation they transformed the face of its reigning icon.

Glaciers form when winter snowfall exceeds summer melt. As layers of snow build up on a mountain's slopes, they compress beneath the weight of the overriding snowpack. Air is driven from deeper layers and snow solidifies into ice. Under pressure the ice becomes plastic; yielding to the pull of gravity, it flows downhill as a glacier. As glaciers drag against bedrock

Emmons Glacier *Largest of Rainier's glaciers, the Emmons is also the largest in the continental United States. Its intricate pattern of crevasses reflects the movement of hundreds of feet of ice over a broken topography of ridges, knobs, and cliffs.*

Mirror Lakes, evening light *Much of the park's rolling subalpine parkland reflects a glacial heritage. Cirques, tarns, moraines, and glacier-smoothed ridges echo the sculpting work of ice.*

they loosen and pluck angular blocks and pieces of rock. Using these as a rasp, they cut and scrape away at the surface beneath them. Over thousands of years they act as gigantic belt sanders, grinding down slopes, widening river valleys, and undercutting intervening ridges and peaks. Given Mount Rainier's heavy snow load and loosely structured volcanic rock, its glaciers had a field day.

Glaciers wrapped the mountain in a mantle of ice on at least two occasions during the last glaciation. Alpine glaciers from high on the mountain also merged with the Cordilleran ice sheet that carved Puget Sound. Even Rainier's southernmost glacier, which was most exposed to summer melting, pushed 65 miles down the Cowlitz River valley. In what amounts to a geological heartbeat glaciers gouged and quarried the mountain's slopes, transforming its youthful contours into the rough and haggard visage we know today. When the climate warmed at the close of the Pleistocene, Rainier's glaciers drew back to their mountain cirques. The volcano may have stood close to 16,000 feet in elevation then, but it had lost a third

of its mass to the ravages of ice. The remnants of Gibraltar Rock and Little Tahoma suggest something of the mountain's former girth, but its undoing was far from complete.

GLACIERS MAY BE THE MOST PERSISTENT EROSIVE AGENTS at work on Mount Rainier, but they are hardly the most dramatic. That distinction goes to the volcanic mudflows geologists call lahars. These are avalanches of rock, mud, and ice that race down a volcano's flanks and bury lowland valleys. All of Rainier's volcanic traits lend themselves to mudflows: its loosely layered, downsloping rocks, its overriding mantle of snow and ice, its conduit of steam vents and constant internal heat. Snow- and icemelt percolate down through the volcano's rocky strata continually. Meltwaters become heated and are transformed into an acidic brew that cooks and chemically alters rocks in the volcano's core. The result is something approaching a claylike torte. Anyone who has ventured very high on Rainier's rock cleavers or explored its summit craters has had a taste of this stuff. The process continues for centuries or millennia as glaciers scrape the outer rocks exposing the chemically weakened core. Then an eruption, or an earthquake, or nothing more than the persistent pull of gravity causes part of the mountain to shear and collapse.

Sunset Amphitheater, Puyallup Glacier *Even in post-glacial time, the mountain continues to deconstruct. About five hundred years ago the Electron Mudflow surged from high on the mountain's western shoulder and buried much of the Puyallup River valley to a depth of 60 feet.*

About 5,600 years ago Rainier was wracked by a collapse that altered the shape of Puget Sound. Evidence of eruptions at the time suggest that volcanic activity may have triggered the event, but whatever the cause, the top 2,000 feet of the summit—almost three-quarters of a cubic mile of rock, clay, and ice—collapsed and avalanched down the northeast slope of the mountain at speeds exceeding 100 miles an hour. Lubricated by wet clay and melted ice, a churning tidal wave the consistency of wet cement engulfed the Winthrop and Emmons glaciers, overtopped Steamboat Prow, and boiled down the West Fork and White River valleys swallowing everything in its path.

The Osceola Mudflow, as it is now called, converged north of the present park boundary and churned west down the White River valley, burying the townsite of Greenwater and filling the valley floor

hundreds of feet deep. It exploded out of the mountain front and spread out over the Puget Sound lowland, covering more than 125 square miles. Within hours the mudflow buried the present sites of Enumclaw, Buckley, Kent, Auburn, Sumner, and Puyallup beneath as much as 70 feet of the old summit before filling in an arm of Puget Sound several miles long—a distance of more than 65 miles from the peak. The depression the Osceola left on the mountain, defined by Gibraltar Rock, Point Success, and Liberty Cap, is nearly 2 miles in diameter. Clearly visible from east of the mountain today, it suggests the dimensions of one of the largest mudslides the world has known.

Catastrophic as it was, the Osceola was not an isolated event. Geologists studying the mountain have found evidence of more than sixty mudflows in the last ten thousand years. Major flows inundate lowlands on average every five hundred to one thousand years. Smaller lahars sweep down the mountain much more frequently. Both have affected every major valley in the park. About the same time the Osceola broke loose, a large mudflow 1,000 feet deep careened down the

Moss, sedges, and boulders, Summerland *Angular boulders that turn high meadows into Japanese rock gardens are often deposited by volcanic mudflows. Over the past thousand years, more than sixty such lahars have affected* 84 *every major valley in the park.*

south side of the mountain, engulfing Paradise in a wave of rubble and scattering rocks and debris over the top of Mazama Ridge. The lahar continued down the Paradise and upper Nisqually rivers before coming to rest around the present site of Ashford. The large angular boulders scattered around Paradise and along the trail to Panorama Point are remnants of its passage.

Other mudflows are much more recent. About five hundred years ago, a slope failure in Sunset Amphitheater on the mountain's west face sent a roiling wave of mud and rock down the Puyallup River. The Electron Mudflow buried the present town site of Orting beneath 15 feet of wet rubble and covered 14 miles of Puget lowlands. Geologists studying this recent lahar have found no evidence that it was triggered by an eruption. This raises serious safety concerns. Unlike volcanic eruptions, which are generally preceded by swarms of earthquakes, potentially destructive lahars may give no warning at all. Today towns like Orting, Ashford, Packwood, and Enumclaw, as well as wide swaths of Tacoma and Seattle, sit directly in the tracks of future mudflows. The proximity of a large population to the kinds of hazards posed by Mount Rainier makes it the most dangerous of Cascade volcanoes. In light of the events that followed the eruption of Mount Saint Helens, in which fifty-seven people lost their lives, scientists from the U.S. Geological Survey and the University of Washington closely monitor the volcano. At the same time U.S.G.S. scientists and Park

Service officials are working to educate area residents and park visitors about the potential hazards posed by Mount Rainier. Nearby Pierce County has factored these hazards into its zoning codes, and evacuation plans have been adopted by some local communities. It may be centuries before another slope failure sends a wall of mud crashing down the slopes of the volcano, but geologists have no doubt it will happen.

In the meantime the mountain has not slacked off in its volcanic upkeep. In fact it ranks second in seismic activity in the Cascades; only Mount Saint Helens is more volatile. Rainier has tossed off four major eruptions in the last 3,000 years alone. Around 2,500 years ago a renewed cycle of eruptive activity began to rebuild the summit cone. Eruptions sent hot ash and gobs of lava cascading down its western slopes and showered blankets of pumice over Yakima Park. Andesite flows filled the floor of the shattered caldera and built up a young volcanic cone 1,000 feet above the crater rim, just as Saint Helens is doing today. Subsequent eruptions formed a second small summit crater. The high point where the crater rims converge is Columbia Crest.

The mountain has been quiet over the past century or so, but geologists have found evidence of at least one eruption during historical time. Thin layers of pumice on moraines left by receding glaciers indicate volcanic activity between 1820 and 1854; the dates were calculated from tree ring counts. Scientists have found no evidence of many later reported eruptions, though steam rising from the summit could account for many historical "sightings." More recently, a series of steam explosions commenced in the 1960s, and new steam vents opened on Gibraltar Rock and above the Kautz and South Tahoma glaciers. Steam vents around the summit craters are still hot and active, but the most dramatic events on the mountain in recent decades have come from its erosive undoing.

In 1947 heavy runoff from a fall rainstorm became dammed behind a section of the Kautz Glacier high on the mountain's southern slope. When it broke loose it sent a wall of mud and boulders down Kautz Creek, destroying miles of valley-bottom forest, washing out a highway bridge, and burying the road to

Autumn, Stevens Canyon *Lava flows from the Mount Rainier volcano filled surrounding river canyons during Pleistocene time. Today andesitic lava forms several prominent ridges emanating from the mountain, including this cliff and talus slope below Martha Falls.*

Longmire beneath 30 feet of debris. The Kautz was a small mudflow by Rainier's standards. An avalanche triggered by a slope failure on Little Tahoma Peak sixteen years later was more in keeping with the mountain's scale. In December of that year a massive rock slide avalanched nearly 2,000 feet down the sheer north face of Little Tahoma and onto the steep slope of the Emmons Glacier. The slide, carrying pieces of the mountain the size of buildings, swept down the glacier with such speed that it shot out over its terminus, leaving a small stream-gauging station untouched. The wall of rocks careened down the valley like a nightmarish freight train, scouring side slopes hundreds of feet high before coming to rest a half mile above White River campground. The lower slopes of Emmons Glacier still lay buried beneath its rubble.

The Kautz and Emmons events were punctuations on the page of the mountain's unraveling. The ongoing text of Rainier's erosion can be read throughout the park; a vivid passage is currently unfolding along the upper West Side Road. For more than a decade flood-triggered debris flows have swept down Tahoma Creek from South Tahoma Glacier on almost a yearly basis. Since 1986 outburst floods have carved a gorge 130 feet deep below the glacier, toppled forest trees, and dumped boulders, mud, and debris into the valley below at a rate of a foot and a half per year. Debris flows have buried a picnic area, obliterated parts of the West Side Road, and closed the lower Tahoma Creek trail. The floods show little sign of abating.

These days upper Tahoma Creek is not as easy to get to as it once was, and it presents a raw and somewhat ravaged sight once reached. But like the recovering forests of Kautz Creek or the fresh moraines below Nisqually Glacier, it offers a first-hand glimpse of the geologic processes that continue to shape this restless landscape.

Weathered snags and young trees, Kautz Creek *The 1947 Kautz Creek Mudflow, which crossed the Nisqually road below Longmire, is one of the most recent and easily seen on the mountain. Geological process remains an ongoing event at Mount Rainier.*

 **Unicorn and Foss Peaks, Tatoosh Range**
A large body of molten rock pushed up beneath the surface of the present park around twelve million years ago and underlies most of the park today. It formed a lovely, granite-like rock called granodiorite that is exposed along the Tatoosh Range and Sunrise Ridge.

Chapter Three

ISLAND WILDERNESS
The Weave of Mountain Life

The weather was too good to leave the mountain. I had just spent a starlit night camped on Meany Crest high above Summerland, and a splendid day on Little Tahoma Peak. The view to the north, over the massive ice fields of the Emmons and Winthrop glaciers, was spectacular. The white and rippled sea of ice was cloven by the rock face of Steamboat Prow, and the humped rise of Burroughs Mountain trailed in its wake like an island. My climbing partner had to return to a job in Seattle that night, a bludgeonlike end to an exquisite mountain ramble, but I had arranged for a

stay of execution. The following dawn found me sipping tea from my thermos as the first rays of light washed over Sunrise.

At 6,400 feet in elevation, Sunrise is among the most dramatic settings in Mount Rainier National Park. A view of the mountain from the meadows of Yakima Park takes in the magnitude of the upper Emmons Glacier as it spills steeply from the summit. Curtis Ridge and Little Tahoma hem the ice in steep lava cliffs, and the gentle rise of Burroughs Mountain lifts like an escalator to the sky. Finishing off the last of

my tea and grabbing a light day pack, I started up the Burroughs Mountain trail for a leisurely day of what my old friend Mark Twain once dubbed "alpine pedestrianism." True alpine, the life zone above the upper limit of tree growth, is scarce in the Pacific Northwest. Our mountains are generally lower than the interior ranges, and ice and permanent snowfields tend to dominate their upper reaches. Mount Rainier offers the most generous expanse of arctic alpine terrain in the Cascades, but even here most of it is confined to the steep upper ridges and narrow rock cleavers that separate the mountain's glaciers. The rolling, plateau-like summit of Burroughs Mountain presents some of the most accessible and diverse alpine tundra in the park, and early that Monday morning I had it all to myself.

The trail led up and around the north side of the mountain, one of the massive lava flows that Rainier laid down during a pulse of ice-age glaciation. I crossed a lingering north-side snowfield—a faint hint of that forgotten age—and wound my way up past the last wind-twisted *krummholz* trees and on to the ridge

top. At first glance, the broad summit of Burroughs Mountain has the look of a stony desert. Compared to the lush meadows of Paradise, or even Summerland, it seems almost stark. Much of the ground was bare volcanic soil and rock, and what vegetation there was seemed a pale and sickly gray-green. This is partly due to Burroughs's position in the rainshadow of the mountain, and partly to its downwind accumulation of nutrient-poor pumice soils. But the nature of these plants is primarily a function of altitude. At an elevation of more than 7,000 feet, these thin, low clumps and trailers of vegetation are typical of the high alpine zone elsewhere on the mountain. More than that, these small, somewhat inconspicuous plants are wonderfully adapted to the harsh, stressful conditions that prevail at these elevations year-round.

A closer look among the scattered stones revealed a stunning garden in miniature. Alpine plants have developed remarkable strategies for survival in environments that the most persistent of gardeners would dismiss out of hand. All are small and short-stemmed, and grow close to the ground in cushions,

 Tipsoo Lake, Governors Ridge, and the mountain *Mount Rainier National Park offers a rich diversity of habitats—from snow-swept ridges above treeline to stunning subalpine parklands and valley forests—and hosts an abundance of wildlife species.*

rosettes, or mats. Their low profiles offer little resistance to severe mountain winds and help protect plant tissues from abrasion by wind-borne pumice and ice. Nearly all alpine plants are perennials, economizing on the energy needed to produce new plant parts each year. Many begin growing at temperatures hovering just above freezing, and they accommodate the brief, intense summer season by flowering and setting seed in much less time than lowland plants. The leaves of some are thick and waxy like those of desert plants and the leaves and stems of most are furred with tiny hairs, giving them their pale gray-green cast.

Mountain dwellers
A mountain goat kid, vine maple leaf after an early snowfall, and false hellebore and wild strawberry leaves in frost.

93

Mount Rainier's alpine zone, *the extent of land above the growth of trees, presents the harshest environment in the Pacific Northwest. Yet horned larks, water pipits, and rosy finches breed there, while pikas, heather voles, and white-tailed ptarmigans reside there year-round.*

94

These fleecy coats help insulate them from the cold (it can snow or freeze at anytime during the growing season) and help them trap blowing dust to build up needed soil. The hairs also diffuse the harsh ultraviolet rays of summer sunlight, protecting leaf pores and conserving moisture.

What captivates me most about these tough, drought-resistant little plants is their lavish blooms.

Though alpine plants are small their flowers are often full-sized, lending them an extravagant beauty out of proportion to their stature. Among the alpine gems in bloom that day were dense cushions of pink-flowered moss campion, snowy beds of spreading phlox, and sky-blue polemonium. A patch of golden fleabane winked beside purple-blue trumpets of Davidson's penstemon, and clumps and ribbons of sweet-smelling Lyle's lupine wound across the hilltop. Creamy tufts of partridgefoot interspersed with the slender stars of Tolmie's saxifrage (first discovered by the intrepid Scot on the other side of the mountain). Some of the plants in Rainier's rainshadow are not found on the west side of the mountain; having traveled from east of the Cascades during the warm dry period that followed the ice age, they are better adapted to the drier east side. Scattered tufts of green-leaf fescue suggest the eastern Washington plateau country, and feathered traces of lichen round out one of the most intricate and beautiful alpine gardens anywhere in the Northwest.

Slopes littered with scattered stones, or

"fellfields," like the broad shoulders of Burroughs Mountain are critical habitats for alpine plants. Fellfields extend well up the mountain's highest ridges, and, rather than hindering plant growth, stones create microsites necessary for alpine plants to flourish. Rainier's high exposed ridges are often blown free of snow by late winter. Stones shelter plants from the lacerating and drying effects of harsh mountain winds while trapping soil particles and moisture-providing snow. In summer the modicum of shade they provide helps conserve moisture and keep plant roots cool. When stones are removed (as they frequently were by the quarryload by early climbing parties building windbreaks) erosion sets in, frost and needle ice break up the soil, plant roots are exposed and plants are lost. Researchers working in the alpine areas of the park have found that only a few alpine plant species are able to reestablish in stone-free areas.

As the trail drops down a shallow slope, scattered patches of heather appear, their deep evergreen foliage and pink, ivory, and yellow bells ring brightly against the pumice soil. Heather meadows flourish in areas

~ **Christine Falls, winter** *Winter lies heavily over Mount Rainier, underscoring its early description as an arctic island in a temperate forest. While high-country lakes remain locked under snow and ice, rivers and streams continue to churn past ice-rimed rocks.*

where snow stays put in winter and lingers late into spring and summer. Like other alpine communities on the mountain, they too originate in fellfields. Their short scaly or needlelike leaves also capture windblown dust and ash, and bits of organic matter carried from below. As branches spread and take root in newly captured soils, older parts of the plant die back and become buried. Studies have shown that even though heathers flower profusely, seedlings and young plants are rarely found in mature heather communities, suggesting these plants do not reproduce often by seed. By dating ash layers, the University of Washington's Ola Edwards discovered that volcanic soils have been accumulating in some of these communities for more than six thousand years. Beneath the ash she found old fellfields containing pollen and stems that dated to seven thousand years. All this suggests to Dr. Edwards that some of these heathers have been growing con-tinuously for at least seven if not ten thousand years, when the glaciers last receded from these slopes. If this is the case, some of Mount Rainier's heathers may

rank among the oldest living things on earth.

Ironically, some of the oldest heather and fellfield communities are located in alpine areas that receive the heaviest human use. The corridor from Panorama Point to Camp Muir is of particular concern to park managers because of the large number of visitors who use it daily during the summer season. Climbers intent on reaching Camp Muir stick pretty much to the trail, but increasing numbers of day hikers follow the route part way then wander off the trail and across sensitive alpine slopes. Plants that for thousands of years have adapted to eruption and ashfall, avalanche and ice storm easily succumb to repeated trampling and the resulting erosion. Other high, exposed ridges like Ptarmigan and Curtis allow little room on their narrow crests for both plants and climbers' trails and camps. This is especially unfortunate as these high ridges may be critical links in the distribution of alpine plants from one part of the mountain to the next.

An equally specialized but more mobile and adaptable community also inhabits the alpine world.

Winter trees *The park's subalpine trees have adapted superbly to the severe conditions that prevail in the upper forest. Subalpine fir's spire–like shape and short flexible limbs shed heavy snow easily. Their lower limbs, pressed flat beneath the snowpack, can take root and sprout, giving trees an alternate reproductive strategy.*

97

Cirrus clouds, morning light *Weather patterns shape Mount Rainier's ecosystems. The mountain's west side, which catches the brunt of wet coastal weather, harbors damp, mossy forests and lush subalpine meadows. The park's east-side meadows are drier and support plants from east of the Cascade crest.*

Most of Rainier's alpine animals escape severe winter conditions by migrating to warmer sites, but a few have developed strategies for surviving here year-round. In late spring and early summer, horned larks, water pippits, and rosy finches arrive to nest and raise their young in the park's alpine tundra. White-tailed ptarmigans, the only birds that reside year-round in the alpine zone, are equipped with downy, feathered "snowshoe" feet. Ptarmigans shift from winter white to mottled brown as they cluck through summer vegetation for seeds and leaves. Clucking around among the heathers myself (and scaring up only an occasional bumblebee), I find the neat, trimmed-back tunnels of heather voles, though the little gray-brown mouse herself eludes me. Heather voles and a few other small mammals have learned to thrive in harsh alpine conditions, feeding on seeds, lichens, and berries, and sporting thick pelts of fur. They raise their young during the brief weeks of summer but remain active year-round in tunnels beneath the snow. Though their tunnelings crisscross the alpine slopes, it's rare that I ever see a heather vole. Much

more easily found are pikas. These small, plump, round-eared members of the rabbit family live year-round in colonies in the park's high rock slides and talus slopes. Unlike heather voles, pikas are noisy, conspicuous, and frenetically active throughout the day. Ever watchful for predators like hawks and coyotes, they scurry from rock piles to nearby meadows to gather plants. Some of their harvest is spread over warm rocks to dry. Stored in miniature haystacks beneath large overhanging rocks, these caches see them through the winter.

While pikas monopolize talus slopes, the cliffs above are the province of the park's largest alpine mammal, the mountain goat. During summer bands of mountain goats range high on the mountain's upper slopes, where they effortlessly traverse steep snowfields, glaciers, and cliffs to feed on the sparse growth of mountain plants. Their muscular shoulders and soft, split hooves are superbly adapted to narrow ledges and cliff faces, and their thick white coats give them the appearance of snow patches on a far rock. Distant, reclusive, and implacable, no other animal is more

Hoary marmot, Spray Park *A signature species of the park's subalpine meadows, marmots have adapted to their mountain world by fattening up on summer plant growth for their long hibernations through the months of snow.*

symbolic of the rugged splendor of the high Cascades. They embody the wholeness of the mountain realm, a creature inseparable from its alpine world.

IN CONTRAST TO THE HARSH LAND ABOVE THE TREES, THE subalpine meadows that necklace the volcano offer habitats lush with livability. John Muir, a naturalist intimate with mountain landscapes of the West, called them "the lower gardens of Eden." Deep winter snows blanket the upper forests and meadowlands throughout the winter, and summer snowmelt waters a rich mosaic of woodland, garden, rivulet, and lake. Among the

first signs of life coaxing spring into the high meadows—after the noisy return of gray jays and Clark's nutcrackers—are the tracks of marmots bounding across the snowdrifts. These largest and shaggiest members of the ground squirrel clan are a handsome gray above darkening to nearly black below, with dark brown tails. Rainier's hoary marmots wake from their winter-long hibernations in May of most years and tunnel up through deep snow to greet the summer season head-on. Their waking strikes visitors to the late spring meadows as a gradual affair; marmots seem to spend as much time dozing on sun-warmed boulders as feeding and cavorting with each other in their comic and endearing way. As the meadows begin to melt free in June, and subalpine buttercups and western anemones join glacier and avalanche lilies on newly greening hillsides, marmots begin a summer-long feeding binge that will see them plump and ripe for winter sleep by fall.

Hoary marmots live in colonies of extended families in burrows usually dug into glacial moraines. As the summer season progresses and the year's young venture out, I love to watch them chase each other and play-wrestle among the wildflower meadows of Paradise or Sunrise, or on the open slopes below Pinnacle Peak. Older members of the colony share sentry duty on nearby rocks and their shrill alarm whistles, sounded at any approach of danger (golden eagles, cougars, coyotes, and bears all number among their predators), send the entire clan darting for the safety of their burrows. Feeding follows the blooming season as different meadow communities emerge from winter snow. Marmots move from anemones to avalanche lilies, paintbrush to mountain daisies, favoring newly emerging plants with tender, immature flowers but sampling almost anything. By October a few monkeyflowers, shooting stars, and marsh marigolds may linger along streams and seeps, but most of the meadow blooms have withered and died. Marmots have doubled their springtime weight by then and repair to their grass-lined burrows for a long, uneventful sleep. True hibernators, their breathing slows as their heart rate drops to four or five beats a minute and their body temperature cools to a few degrees above

freezing—a neat trick as winter storms swirl a few feet above them.

Marmots' watchful diligence and unmistakable alarm whistles save them from the fate of being a major prey species. Not so their smaller cousins, the golden mantled ground squirrels and yellow-pine chipmunks that share their subalpine world. These two critters,

Mount Rainier and Cathedral Peak from Alpine Lakes Wilderness
Late summer and autumn bring a host of predators to the Cascade high country—hawks, eagles, cougars, bobcats, coyotes, foxes, and weasels, among others.

101

among those most frequently seen by visitors to Rainier's high country, are often confused with each other. Both are brown with black-striped backs, but ground squirrels are slightly larger and lack the prominent eye stripe of the yellow-pines. Ground squirrels also prefer the drier east-side meadows of the park and are more frequently seen around Sunrise and Glacier Basin. Yellow-pine chipmunks are everywhere in the subalpine and feed on almost anything: bugs, seeds, berries, leaves. Unlike ground squirrels they climb the lower limbs of trees to forage. They are not above panhandling, especially at picnic areas and along popular trails, and when that fails they are known to rifle through packs for goodies. Aside from the delight (or chagrin) they bring to hikers, they, along with pocket gophers, voles, and other small mammals, serve as the major prey base for a seasonal confluence of predators that converges on the park's high country in late summer and autumn. Redtail hawks and northern harriers hunt the open meadows, while eagles and sharp-shinned and Cooper's hawks pass through on their southern migrations. Coyotes, bobcats, pine

martens, red foxes, and short-tailed weasels prowl the edges of forest and meadow to grab their share of the season's bounty.

By mid- to late July the subalpine summer is in full bloom, and the high meadows are awash with wild-flowers. In the early morning or evening hours, visitors to the meadows are almost certain to encounter the park's most popular large mammal, Columbian black-tailed deer. Deer are common and abundant throughout the lower forests and are often seen feeding along park roads. But they are at their loveliest knee-deep in the subalpine flower fields. Does are usually accompanied by one or two fawns or yearlings who snap to attention at the approach of a hiker, their large ears rotating like radar dishes. The young, which are born in June, are reddish brown and spotted to blend with the forest floor. Within a month or so they are able to follow their mothers to feeding and watering areas. Fawns are occasionally taken by coyotes in the park, but these predators run the good chance of a thrashing by a protective doe's sharp hooves. A far more effective predator on deer is the cougar. These

Glacier lily emerging through melting snow

*Snowmelt pond, **Spray Park** Subalpine plant communities are keyed to patterns of winter snowmelt. Glacier and avalanche lilies are among the first to bloom in the high meadows, gentians and pearly everlasting among the last. White heather (foreground) prefers stony sites with a relatively late snowmelt.*

Subalpine blooms (Left to right) *Indian paintbrush, pink heather, yellow and pink monkeyflowers, false hellebore with western anemone, and avalanche lily.*

lithe, powerful, and solitary hunters may be the most adept of North American carnivores. They can cover more than 30 feet in a single pounce and can easily take down large prey. With their long incisors and powerful jaws, cougars can with a single bite to the neck suffocate or break the spinal column of a deer or elk. They usually hunt at dawn and dusk and are rarely seen in the park, but their presence is confirmed by the alertness of deer as they venture out of cover to feed.

On the east side of the mountain the summer meadows are host to another large and striking member of the deer family, the elk. Mount Rainier's

elk are impressive. Bulls stand almost 5 feet at the shoulder and can weigh over 800 pounds, more than three times the size of a deer. Their coats are a rich forest brown with buff rump patches and dark tails. Bulls wear dark brown manes and by late summer sport wide spreading racks of antlers. To spot one in a mountain meadow or hear its sharp rutting whistle echoing among the cliffs is a high point of any visit to Mount Rainier, but when the park was established one hundred years ago there were few elk to be found. Commercial and subsistence hunting in the nineteenth century had reduced elk numbers throughout the

Northwest and the earliest explorers to visit the mountain failed to see one. Records exist of small numbers of Roosevelt elk in valleys surrounding the park in the early years of the twentieth century, and between 1912 and 1934 Rocky Mountain elk from the Yellowstone-Teton area were introduced to the vicinity of the park. The imported animals thrived here, may have interbred with resident elk, and soon extended their ranges into the park.

Elk winter in lower valley forests which lie largely outside the park, and there they must contend with human-caused changes in habitat. As a result of heavy clearcutting on forestlands surrounding the park from the 1950s through the 1970s, an abundance of leafy browse became available and elk numbers shot up dramatically. By the late 1970s concern that overgrazing by elk might be damaging the park's high meadows led to close monitoring by biologists. New directives to manage national forests to encourage mature and old-growth habitat, along with careful management by the Washington Department of Fish and Wildlife, should insure that elk populations remain stable. Today

Mount Rainier supports a summer population of 800 to 1,200 elk. They are most easily seen mornings and evenings at Sunrise, Mount Fremont, Mystic Lake, and Shriner Peak. The few elk that venture into the west side of the park stay low in the river valleys and are seldom seen by visitors.

Bugling elk signal the coming of autumn to Rainier's high country just as surely as marmots whistle in the summer. Fall is a spectacular time in the

Bear grass *The spring growth of bear grass is among the early foods favored by black bears as they emerge from hibernation (they also enjoy the roots). Black bears migrate to the park's high meadows in summer to feast on plants and berries. A few are known to have taken shortcuts over the mountain.*

subalpine. Small mammals are everywhere, scooting about gathering stores against the winter, and raptors glide on thermals over the meadows to hunt them. Birds and squirrels rifle the cone crops for seeds, and ravens flap noisily from tree to tree. Nearly all the mountain wildflowers have withered and folded into seed; only an occasional aster, bistort, or gentian hints at the glory of summer. Anemones bow and sway shaggy seed heads in the rising wind and pearly everlasting stays true to its name. But along the edges of the subalpine forest and out into the meadows, the inconspicuous shrubs come into their own as the first frosts ignite them. The leaves of white rhododendrons turn golden at the touch of frost. Nearby mountain ash leaves kindle orange to fiery red, advertising their berries to passing flocks of birds. All around the mountain, meadows transform into waves of purple and scarlet with the autumn flush of huckleberry leaves. Blue-leaf huckleberries are the most prized of mountain berries, and they inevitably reduce me to groveling on all fours as I gather up their sweetness like a bear. More than once I've rounded a bend in a berry

patch to find myself not alone in my foraging.

Black bears flock to the high meadows during berry time, and who can blame them? They become so consumed with lapping up the sweet acres that it is the easiest time to watch them. The meadows of Paradise, Stevens Ridge, and Shriner Peak are favorite spots. Blacker than night, the bears stand out on any mountain slope (though Rainier's black bears can also be cinnamon brown to grizzly tan). Like humans, whom they resemble in many ways, bears are true omnivores, but they lay claim to a much greater catholicity of tastes. They'll eat practically anything: from grubs in rotting logs to shoots, leaves, roots, the inner bark of trees, carrion, fish (they are excellent gaffers), small mammals, fawns, honey—basically, what-ever looks good. Though they may seem sluggish, black bears are extremely powerful and surprisingly fleet of foot; they are best enjoyed (as the posters say) from a distance.

Black bears are mostly solitary and independent, but females become devoted and fiercely protective mothers. They mate briefly in early summer and cubs

Black-tailed deer *Most common of the park's large mammals, deer can be seen at all elevations at Mount Rainier. Many summer in subalpine meadows and a few winter in low-elevation forests outside the park.*

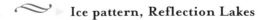 **Ice pattern, Reflection Lakes**

feasts. Fat and shaggy, black bears then head downslope, through the first dustings of snow, for some final munching in the forest (nuts, grubs, spawning fish) before entering their winter dens. Like the last guests at a party, a few bears may range about well into winter, but when snows at last cover the forest floor the bruins' movable feast comes to an end.

Lichen, rock, and mountain from Tolmie Peak *Lichens, one of the most intrepid life forms on the mountain, are found at all elevations, even the summit. They are formed of symbiotic relationships between fungi and algae. The fungus derives organic nutrients from the alga while supplying its water and minerals.*

THE LONG WAY IN TO EUNICE LAKE PROVED LONGER than I had counted on. By the time I reached Ipsut Pass from the Ipsut Creek campground the clear morning skies had been swallowed up by clouds, and a cold wind out of the west carried the taste of rain. My hoped-for view of the mountain from the lake disappeared along with the last of the sky, so I turned back down Ipsut Creek toward camp. I recrossed remnant snow patches as the trail switchbacked down the steep rocky slope and into scattered stands of high forest. In consolation, I remembered that a few of these stands harbor some of the park's oldest trees.

are born in winter while bears are denned up. When they emerge in April, their first order of business is fattening up on grubs, cambium from the inner bark of trees or winterkilled deer and elk. The year's feeding reaches its peak with their communal berry

The upper forest is cut by avalanche tracks and has been ravaged by centuries of winter storms, but a handful of ancient Alaska yellow-cedars cling tenaciously. Soon a large, shaggy yellow-cedar more than six feet through looms up by the trailside; its lacy blue-green boughs rock slowly with the wind. Scientists surveying this basin in the 1970s dated this tree by increment bore at 1,200 years in age—one of the oldest known trees in the park. Other grandfathers rise broken-topped and battered among the scattered stands: ragged yellow-cedars and avalanche-scarred mountain hemlocks, veterans of long-forgotten wars. After the trail crosses the creek, I descend into closed patches of forest more characteristic of the mountain's intermediate slopes.

The dense Pacific silver fir forests that mantle the middle slopes of Mount Rainier carry the feel of winter most of the year. Little sunlight works through the thick canopy of fir and hemlock, and the low mossy growth of the forest floor is perpetually cool and damp. Snow lingers late in these mountain forests, and the drooping lichen-strewn limbs of mountain hemlock and Alaska yellow-cedar add somber texture. Occasionally the gray, checkered bark of a slender,

long-needled western white pine introduces a note of elegance to the montane forest, and stately groves of noble firs hold court along its lower slopes. On the drier east side of the mountain, Engelmann spruce and whitebark pine also enter the picture. But Pacific silver fir remains the dominant mountain tree.

Hardy and extremely tolerant of shade, silver firs can seed in beneath dense forest shade and out-compete most other trees, even shade-tolerant champs like western and mountain hemlock. Eventually, when even the longest-lived trees like yellow-cedars, western redcedars, or Douglas-firs have died out, silver firs may develop into pure climax stands. Even though the trees themselves are not all that old (silver firs seldom live past five hundred years), the communities can be ancient.

On overcast days like this, when clouds and mist sift through the forest, the straight silvery trunks and deep green crowns of silver firs light the dark mountain slopes like softly glowing candles. The floor is a mosaic of huckleberry shrubs and moss. Looking closely where the huckleberries leave off, I find a few

109

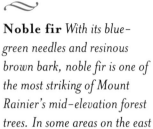

Noble fir *With its blue-green needles and resinous brown bark, noble fir is one of the most striking of Mount Rainier's mid-elevation forest trees. In some areas on the east side of the park, they form continuous stands.*

of the small flowers that thrive in the cool dampness: bunchberry dogwood and rose-colored pipsissewa, pink and white wintergreen and the down-tilted trumpets of twinflower. Their shiny evergreen leaves gleam like coins in the moss.

A Douglas squirrel chatters loudly from a nearby tree, and later a snowshoe hare darts across the trail and disappears. Many of the animals I found in the park's subalpine zone are plentiful here in the upper forest, along with many common to the lower valley

forests. Unfortunately, they are difficult to see in the dense woods. Yellow-pine chipmunks and mantled ground squirrels are as common here as in the subalpine, but here they are also joined by some forest-dwelling cousins: Townsend's chipmunks, northern flying squirrels, and Douglas squirrels, or chickarees. Later in the summer, the silver fir forest becomes a "hardhat-required" worksite as chickarees cut the stout pitchy silver fir cones and let them fall to the ground like bombs. Mice, shrews, and voles are also common here, as are their predators. Long-tailed weasels prowl the woods, and sleek reddish brown pine martens range through the forest canopy in search of small mammals and birds. The snowshoe hare that ducked into the brush had good reason to disappear as well; it is a favorite prey of bobcats, especially here on the west side of the mountain. But like mink, red foxes, and great horned owls, these small spotted felines prefer to hunt at night and are seldom noticed by diurnal types like me.

Miraculously the rain held off, and a couple of hours down from the pass the reappearance of large

Douglas-firs and western hemlocks signals a return to the lowland forest. The canopy here is open and spacious with trees of all sizes filtering the light. Moss and lichens drape the boughs, and kinglets flit through the open spaces. Standing dead trees or snags are scattered widely through the forest, and the lush floor is littered with fallen giants in various stages of mossy decay. Here in the park's lower valleys, where rainfall is plentiful and temperatures moderate, conditions for growth are optimal. Some of these four- and five-foot diameter Douglas-firs are more than five hundred years old, the redcedars possibly older than that. Though it's the large trees that command my attention in the ancient forest, it is the whole of the forest—its open mossy canopy, standing snags, downed logs, and lush ground cover of herbs, shrubs, ferns, and fungi— that make old growth such exceptional habitat.

Snags provide nesting sites for owls, Vaux's swifts, pileated woodpeckers, flying squirrels, chickarees, several species of bats, pine martens, bobcats, and occasional bears. In fact, about a third of the birds common to Northwest forests are known to

New growth, Douglas-fir *One of the most ubiquitous of Northwest trees, Douglas-fir is a disturbance species. It seeds in readily after a fire, windstorm, mudflow, or other disturbance and grows quickly. Douglas-firs can reach considerable age; some at Mount Rainier approach a thousand years.*

Old-growth forest *Mount Rainier is justifiably renowned for its ancient forests. It is the structure of these old-growth forests—snags, downed logs, a multi-layered canopy, and diversity of age and species—that makes them such productive habitats for wildlife. It takes 200 to 250 years for these characteristics to develop.*

forest ecosystem. It takes 200 to 250 years for forests to develop these characteristics. Once they do, some seventy species of birds, thirty small mammals, and twenty amphibians are known to make their home here. Some, such as northern spotted owls, marbled murrelets, Vaux's swifts, and fishers are dependent on old growth; others, like pileated woodpeckers and west-ern goshawks, do well in younger natural forests, pro-vided they have some old-growth characteristics like standing snags and downed logs. At least forty-five wildlife species depend on old-growth and mature forests for their primary habitats. One of the best known—through no fault of its own—is a small, reclusive owl.

Northern spotted owls are quite selective about where they choose to live. They nest in large hollowed-out snags with good surrounding cover. And they have a distinct taste for the northern flying squirrels that inhabit the old-growth canopy. The open, multi-aged canopies of these forests allow spotted owls room to maneuver but not the larger great horned owls which prey on them. Due to their nature as top feeders in

nest in them. Downed logs serve as habitats for a num-ber of small mammals, reptiles, and amphibians, as well as for a host of invertebrates and nitrogen-fixing bacteria that are essential to the nutrient-cycling of the

these forests, owl populations are closely monitored by biologists as indicators of the overall health of the old-growth ecosystem. As old forests fell to clearcutting outside parks and other protected areas over the past century, the number of spotted owls plummeted. Today, less than 10 percent of the Northwest's old-growth forests remain, and northern spotted owls are listed as threatened by the U.S. Fish and Wildlife Service.

The protected forests of Mount Rainier provide nearly 100,000 acres of excellent habitat for a number of old growth-dependent species, including a healthy population of spotted owls. Mating and nesting in early spring, spotted owls breed every other year in the western Cascades. The young fledge in late spring or early summer, but their rate of mortality is extremely high. Great horned owls are not their only predators; non-native barred owls can nest in second-growth as well as old-growth forests and are making rapid inroads into spotted owl habitat in the Northwest where they also compete for prey. Young owls may have to leave the park to find habitat. Those dispersing to

the south and east of the park stand the best chance of finding breeding habitat; those heading north or west are likely to encounter miles of logged-over forests. For spotted owls and other old growth-dependent species, Mount Rainier is indeed an island.

Among the many challenges facing Mount Rainier National Park in its second century, one of the greatest is insuring its ecological health. This entails maintaining viable populations of all of the park's native species in the face of changing conditions outside park boundaries, as well as restoring and protecting habitats that have been damaged by excessive human use. To do

 Burl, nurse log, and forest, Grove of the Patriarchs

this requires bold new initiatives and working partnerships between the Park Service, other government agencies, the private sector, and, most importantly for Mount Rainier, the people who love it and care about it.

Threats facing the larger ecosystem—which includes both public and private lands surrounding Mount Rainier—are numerous. The park's air quality is affected by urban and industrial pollution upwind of the park. Downstream salmon runs, an important part of the park's riverine ecosystems, are impacted by hydroelectric dams and logging. Winter range for elk, deer, and other wildlife that must leave the park

Forest dwellers (Left to right) *Autumn scene of bunchberry, vine maple, and mushrooms, corydalis, deer fern fiddleheads, and bunchberry dogwood.*

115

during winter is succumbing to development in adjacent valleys, and wildlife dispersal corridors to other protected forest areas have been fragmented by roads and clearcuts. A study published in 1987 found that seven wildlife species present when the park was created were missing from the park. White-tailed ptarmigans are in decline in the high meadows and nesting marbled murrelets, a federally threatened species, are few in the park's lower forest. At the same time some non-native species like barred owls are becoming more numerous at Mount Rainier, and non-native trout, introduced to some of the park's high lakes decades ago, are thriving at the expense of native amphibians.

The good news is that things are turning around. Some species once believed to have been extirpated from the park appear to be making a comeback. River otters have been spotted in several valleys and at a few high lakes, and fishers, the large sable-furred hunters of the valley forests, which are disappearing across the Northwest, are being seen with increasing frequency. Even the grizzly bear, a species not known to have

existed in the park, made a surreptitious appearance a few years ago, leaving its unmistakable track in a west-side valley just outside the park.

The long-term future of these and many other animals will depend on cooperation between park managers and the managers of state, federal, and private forestlands adjoining the park. This kind of ecosystem management isn't easy. It requires close cooperation between agencies with differing mandates, sharing of scientific data, cooperative planning, continual monitoring, and feedback to decision makers. Fortunately, Mount Rainier National Park has already broken ground in this area. For decades the park has coordinated efforts with surrounding national forests, the Washington Department of Fish and Wildlife, area tribes, and neighboring timber companies on forest management concerns and on issues surrounding elk and deer. In 1995 the Park Service participated in a permitting process involving a nearby coal-fired power plant known to have been the source of between one-third and one-half of the sulfur dioxide polluting the park's air. The agreement that

Dawn, Reflection Lake
The purity of the park's air and waters, the health of its plant and wildlife communities, depends on activities outside its borders. Those who care about the future of Mount Rainier during the park's second century must concern ourselves with the health of the larger ecosystem of which it is a part.

followed will reduce the plant's emissions by 90 percent and should set a precedent for protecting air quality in national parks. Other Park Service efforts have established broad partnerships involving cooperation with businesses, foundations, and citizens' groups. Already these are making a difference in many places at Mount Rainier.

Beginning in the 1980s park crews and volunteers began the long-term work of restoring trampled subalpine meadows. Crisscrossing the meadows were countless "social trails," where hikers cut between established trails, and rest spots and overlooks were beaten down to bare earth. Elsewhere, decades-old scars from misplaced developments still marred subalpine areas. Restoration efforts involved stabilizing eroding slopes, filling in gullies with soil and rock, and replanting native vegetation. The park's approach combined site work with visitor education. Seeds were gathered from nearby meadows, germinated and nursed in a park greenhouse, and thousands of plants were hand planted, largely with the help of volunteer crews.

Narada Falls in fog *"Narada" is said to mean pure or uncontaminated. Descending from Paradise Glacier through the snow and flower fields of Paradise, the falls remains true to its name, which was given to the cascade in 1893 by a member of the Theosophical Society of Tacoma.*

The effort was phenomenally successful. By the end of the decade restoration work was extended to backcountry sites. By the late 1980s the program had grown to a more than quarter-million-dollar operation and the park took on the revegetation of the old Paradise campground. But even with this level of commitment, crews were unable to scratch the surface of the mother of all restoration projects, the old automobile campground at Sunrise. Constructed in the early 1930s during the boom years of park development, the Sunrise campground was a warren of roads and campsites cut by steam shovel into the sloping 6,400-foot meadowlands of Yakima Park. In 1973 the site was closed to cars, and an initial effort was made at revegetating roads and campsites. But damage to the meadows was on a scale beyond the abilities of volunteers armed with spades and trowels. In 1997 a grant from Canon USA and the involvement of the Washington National Guard and others allowed the park to begin an ambitious multi-year restoration project. Mechanized crews removed old roadbeds and restored the slope to its original contours, and volun-

teers began the Herculean task of planting tens of thousands of meadow plants. Early results are promising as work progresses on what is surely the most ambitious subalpine meadow restoration in the Northwest.

Projects like this point the way into the park's second century. Whether restoring meadows or

Paradise Park *Concerted efforts by the Park Service and volunteers to restore damaged meadows over the past two decades have been one of the biggest successes at Mount Rainier.*

119

120

*∼***Silver Falls** (above) *is among the loveliest of the park's many waterfalls, as much for its quiet approach through the Ohanapecosh Valley forest as its thundering presence.* **Ohanapecosh River** (top left) *and* **Carbon River** (bottom left).

rehabilitating trails, volunteers are making a difference at Mount Rainier. In fact over the last twenty-five years of the park's history, volunteers have taken on an increasingly prominent role in caring for the park and serving its visitors. Volunteers in the Parks (or "VIPs" as they're aptly called) have undertaken a broad range of jobs, from meadow restoration and resource work to visitor education, trail and campsite rehabilitation, scientific monitoring, and hosting at park campgrounds. Conservation and outdoor groups as diverse as The Mountaineers, Sierra Club, Mount Rainier National Park Associates, Student Conservation Association, Boy and Girl Scout organizations, and the YMCA have provided the people-power to complete needed projects throughout the park. Volunteer groups from Japan and Europe helped develop handicap-accessible trails and campsites. Even crew members from the Navy's USS *Rainier* have pitched in. In recent years a number of employee groups from area businesses have joined the effort, their members spending weekends and vacations working at Mount Rainier. Volunteer members of the Mountain Rescue

Edith Creek, Paradise Park *Like the park's visitors a century ago, most visitors today head for Paradise. As the number of people entering Mount Rainier each year tips past the two million mark, managers face the difficult task of protecting park resources while insuring continued public enjoyment.*

Council assist with rescues, and in winter members of the Washington Ski Touring Club patrol the ski trails at Paradise. The hours volunteers have put in at the park doubled from a total of twenty-five thousand in

121

The mountain and
forest, Nisqually Valley

1992 to more than fifty thousand in 1997. In the assessment of one park manager, volunteers have become the backbone of park operations.

While hundreds of individuals and organizations step forward to shoulder some of the work of maintaining Mount Rainier National Park, thousands more have ponied up financial contributions. Since the early 1980s congressional appropriations for the Park Service have consistently failed to keep up with either increased visitation to the parks or with inflation. In 1992 the superintendents of Mount Rainier and Olympic national parks responded to the shortfall by securing a grant from the National Parks Foundation to seed a nonprofit organization, the goal of which was to help fund projects aimed at restoring, enhancing, and preserving Washington's national parks. Since then the Mount Rainier, North Cascades & Olympic Fund has raised over a quarter-million dollars from individuals, foundations, and corporate donors. Contributions have helped bring about much-needed educational and research work as well as resource protection and visitor services at Mount Rainier. Among

the projects supported by the Fund are meadow restoration at Paradise and historic restorations of the Tolmie Peak fire lookout and the White River patrol cabin, which will be an interpretive museum presenting the story of the Wonderland Trail. The Fund has helped produce educational videos and interpretive roadside exhibits and helped initiate a volunteer emergency roadside assistance program which has come to the aid of hundreds of stranded visitors. Each August the Fund holds a fundraiser at Mount Rainier. Volunteers greet visitors at entrance stations, provide information about the Fund's activities, and accept donations. All contributions are earmarked for projects at the park.

Close to 2.2 million visitors drove through Mount Rainier's entrance stations in 1995. That's roughly ten people per acre, not terribly crowded, even by Northwest standards. The problem is nearly all of us go to the same few places. Some popular destinations in the park are reaching carrying capacity; a few may have passed it. A pressing issue facing the park, and a focus of its current management plan, is how to insure the continued enjoyment of Mount Rainier by increasing numbers of visitors while protecting the resources they come to see as well as the quality of their experience.

On sunny weekends in summer, cars and vans circle the parking lot at Paradise like jets over La Guardia awaiting clearance to land. Similar conditions prevail at Sunrise and Mowich Lake. Popular day-use trails along the Muir corridor and in the Spray Park and Sunrise areas are crowded by almost anyone's standard, and high meadows continue to be damaged by careless off-trail tramping. As park managers plan for the coming decades, they face not only the prospect of considerably more of us but also the fact that we all expect something slightly different from our visits. Backpackers seek solitude and a sense of pristine wilderness. Climbers are less fussy about other parties on the mountain but want access to high camps and routes. Day hikers relish the freedom to wander off on any trail that catches their fancy. Drivers and sightseers expect uncongested roads and room to stop at scenic pullouts. And everyone wants a parking space at

Carbon River valley from the Clearwater Wilderness *In 1984 Congress granted protection to 200,000 acres of roadless Forest Service lands adjoining Mount Rainier by creating the Clearwater, William O. Douglas, Tatoosh, and Glacier View wilderness areas.*

Paradise. What's more, we bristle at the suggestion that we give any of these things up.

Solutions to these and other issues will of necessity involve trade-offs. Shuttle buses will help reduce congestion but might limit options for driving wherever we like. Limits placed on crowded day-use areas may dampen spontaneity but might improve the quality of visitors' experiences. Closures of flood-ravaged roads would curb auto access but enable money spent on yearly repairs to be redirected to more pressing needs. One of the most critical roles the Park Service will serve in Mount Rainier's second century is education. Once visitors become aware of the damage off-trail tramping or illegal camping inflicts on park ecosystems, they usually comply with regulations. Spring skiers will be less likely to picnic on islands of heather, and snowboarders may think twice before swooshing off snowbanks onto newly emerging meadows. When campers know that White River and Cougar Rock campgrounds sit squarely in the tracks of historic mudflows, they can make informed decisions on where to spend the night.

Autumn, Stevens Canyon *Autumn comes early to the park's high forests and slopes. Huckleberry leaves begin to turn in the high meadows by late August. By the end of September most years, Stevens Canyon is a collage of fall colors.*

Each new window of understanding enriches our appreciation of this wondrously complex environment, and our deepened awareness in turn helps protect it. Ultimately, it is up to all of us who care for Mount Rainier National Park to continue the protection begun by a handful of mountain enthusiasts a century ago.

THE LOW CLOUDS THAT HUNG OVER EATONVILLE BEGAN splattering my windshield with rain by Ashford. At Paradise I ducked into the Jackson Visitor Center hoping thinly for a break in the weather. Finally, acknowledging the inevitable, I climbed into rain gear and marched stoically through blowing fog toward Glacier Vista. Storm-battered trees emerged from the clouds like tattered beggars. Trailside flowers twirled wildly in the wind. As I hunkered down at the overlook, a smudge of light broke through the overcast. It might have been the sun, but it was gone before I could tell for sure. When I left the park two days later, I hadn't *seen* the mountain.

After years of such meteorological reticence on

Autumn reflection, Louise Lake

125

Huckleberry leaves and weathered wood, Stevens Canyon (above) and **subalpine country, Chinook Pass** (right)

Park to the deep shade of the old-growth forests that cloak the mountain's lower slopes and valleys. Hidden among Mount Rainier's lower creeks and river valleys are some of the most magnificent forests in the Pacific Northwest.

Rainier's forests evolved amidst a cacophony of violent natural disturbances—eruptions, mudflows, avalanches, windstorms, wildfires, floods—yet they evoke a timelessness and quiet that belie the ash- and flood-deposited soils they root in. Along sheltered river valleys and in folds of the volcano's cloud-shrouded slopes are groves of trees that have been tasting the rain for ten centuries.

The winter of 1996–97 dumped near-record snows on the mountain. By early June most of the park was still buried, and clouds filled the Puget Sound basin for weeks. Conditions were perfect! I packed rain gear and a thermos and headed off to Mount Rainier. I hoped to find something of the mountain's power and mystery in the shade of its ancient forests.

Passing through the Nisqually entrance station and entering Rainier's old-growth forests after driving

the part of the Northwest's most enigmatic peak, I've begun to look elsewhere than on high for a glimpse of the volcano's prowess. More and more, I'm drawn downward, below the meadows of Paradise and Spray

through miles of cutover second growth is like a drink of mountain snowmelt after a long dry climb. Massive Douglas-firs rise like pillars into a pale and distant sky, their furled lichen-flecked bark glows reddish brown in the shadows. Western redcedars lean on flaring bases and droop lacy green boughs like scarves. Vine maples and sword ferns gather pools of green muted light, and mossy logs lie like beached ships amid carpets of vanilla leaf, huckleberry, and oak fern. As I round the curves trees step close to the road edge like sentries along the way to the palace.

Soon I notice a string of cars stacked up behind me, anxious to get up into the clouds no doubt. So I pull over beside a particularly striking Douglas-fir and let the traffic stream by. Earlier pilgrims have worn a path to the old giant, and I follow, circling its massive ten-foot trunk and gazing up nine or ten stories to the tree's first limbs. Its top, that far again, is lost in the surrounding canopy. The traffic has quieted and the sound of the Nisqually River drifts up through the forest. The silence fills me like a deep pool.

Just up the road I am lured off on the Twin Firs

Morning light, Reflection Lake

Douglas-fir, vine maple, and lichens, Backbone Ridge *When the first snows blanket the upper meadows, deer and elk return to the shelter of lower forests. Old-man's-beard and other lichens form an important part of their winter diets. The lichens are not that high in food value themselves, but they help animals absorb nutrients from other winter foods.*

130

an original forest—though stunted by the poor nature of mudflow soils.

Ecologists see natural disturbances such as wildfires, windstorms, and avalanches, and even long-term events like glacier advances and volcanic mudflows, as essential in maintaining forest health. By creating new habitats like snags and downed logs and establishing pockets of early-succession Douglas-fir, disturbances reinvigorate forest ecosystems and help maintain biological diversity. To get a closer look at a forest that has developed under frequent disturbances—in this case by wildfires—I decided to leave the sodden west side of the park and visit the Ohanapecosh Valley in the mountain's rainshadow.

The next morning I drive through clouds to the snowbound junction with the Stevens Canyon road. The skies are low and dark, the mountain hidden, and eight-foot snowbanks loom along the roadsides. Unlike the majority of my fellow travelers, I forsake Paradise and turn eastward toward the promised groves of the Ohanapecosh.

As I descend Stevens Canyon, snowbanks

Stevens Canyon forest
Vine maples and Sitka alders are among the first to colonize rocky talus slopes and slide areas. Full exposure to afternoon sunlight and evening frost intensifies their autumn colors against the subdued greens of the conifer forest.

winnow, and the limbs of Sitka alders reach tentatively for daylight. A little farther down, catkins are dangling, then the first green flush of leaves. Suddenly, it's spring again. Waterfalls boom from melting snowbanks; trilliums bloom, and spirea and paintbrush

Louise Lake and Stevens Ridge *The crimson leaves of mountain ash (foreground) and the darker burgundy of blue-leaf huckleberries announce the presence of ripe berries to passing birds. In autumn Rainier's high country is a movable feast for wildlife.*

speckle the hillsides. The clouds lift some and I know the Fates are with me.

The trail to Silver Falls is busy. I pass couples and families: girls holding hands with their moms, boys carrying sticks. A swallowtail butterfly basks by the trailside and the songs of chestnut-backed chickadees filter through the woods. The trees here are smaller than those along the Nisqually River, and I notice fewer snags and downed logs. Occasionally I glimpse a large Douglas-fir through the woods, its lower bark scarred with the telltale char of an old burn. Scientists sleuthing this valley, through soil profiles and tree borings, have found that major wildfires burned here around 250, 700, and 1,000 years ago. Each conflagration destroyed the standing forest, but a few old thick-barked Doug-firs survived to seed the next cycle of forest growth and to stand as witnesses to the valley's fiery past.

I remember an earlier visit to Rainier's Carbon River valley in the far northwest corner of the park. In contrast to the Ohanapecosh, the Carbon is among the wettest of Rainier's lower valleys. Its damp forest,

verdant with mossy Sitka spruces, nurse logs, devil's club, and canopy epiphytes, brought to mind the wet coastal rain forest of my home Olympics—only I was a hundred miles from the ocean.

The Ohanapecosh is running blue-gray, swollen with snowmelt. Streamside maples bob in the wind. Occasionally, I spot the cropped stems of sword fern and huckleberry, evidence of browsing elk. I look for them among the trees but come up empty handed. Soon I arrive at Silver Falls. Charged with meltwater as the mountain sheds its snowpack, the falls are a noisy explosion of boiling whitewater haloed by billowing skirts of spray. I stop and let the cool wind wash over me. The river trail continues on into mountain forests of silver fir, but there is one last lowland forest stand—Mount Rainier's most famous—that I've waited until now to visit.

It is late in the afternoon when I cross the suspension bridge over the Ohanapecosh to the island that harbors the Grove of the Patriarchs. The grove's isolation on an island terrace has helped it escape the wildfires that raked the valley over the past one

Old-growth Douglas-fir, Nisqually Valley

Life thrives on death in the forest. Western hemlock seedlings get a tentative start on a nurse log in the shade of towering Douglas-firs. Unlike Douglas-fir, hemlocks reproduce and grow well in shade. Barring a major disturbance, western hemlocks will eventually replace Douglas-fir as the climax species of the lowland forest.

thousand years. I pass between two immense upturned rootwads, monuments to a past winter storm, and enter a grove of six whiskery redcedars, trees already old when Captain Vancouver first noted the mountain in his log. In those days redcedar was the foundation of the Northwest Coast cultures. Its fibrous cinnamon-brown bark provided clothing, baskets, and mats, its aromatic heartwood house planks, carved boxes, and seagoing canoes. The few ancient redcedar groves that survive echo an earlier way of life here, their pungent scent an ageless perfume. Lacking anything as old as Europe's cathedrals, the ancient groves of Mount Rainier, remnants of a forest that once blanketed the Puget lowlands, are one of our culture's best gifts to posterity, legacies of a world still new to human design.

The sound of the river is muted among the giant trees, and a pair of varied thrushes calls back and forth through the stillness. I join a small group of visitors who are passing beneath the trees and speaking in low tones. We stop to take in a pair of monumental Douglas-firs, then gather at the base of a massive redcedar, as if to partake of its wisdom. It may be the oldest tree in the grove; it is certainly the largest. Its lower bark and knobby buttressed roots have been rubbed smooth by the hands of thousands of visitors— for luck perhaps, or maybe to share some of its immense longevity in the face of overwhelming odds. We linger a long time. When a last elderly couple snaps their picture and wanders off, I place my hand against the cedar's smooth ruddy bark and begin a slow and hopeful stroll about the feet of a master.

∽ The mountain at twilight

REFERENCES

General

Barcott, Bruce. *The Measure of a Mountain: Beauty and Terror on Mount Rainier.* Seattle: Sasquatch Books, 1997. A literate and engaging exploration of Rainier as mountaineering challenge and cultural icon.

Beckey, Fred. *Cascade Alpine Guide I: Columbia River to Stevens Pass.* 2nd ed. Seattle: The Mountaineers, 1987. Definitive guide to climbing routes on the mountain by the legendary Northwest alpinist.

Filley, Bette. *The Big Fact Book about Mount Rainier.* Issaquah, Wash.: Dunamis House, 1996. An encyclopedic compilation of information and lore about Rainier (First dog ascent: 1891!).

Kirk, Ruth. *Sunrise to Paradise: The Story of Mount Raineir National Park.* Seattle: University of Washington Press, forthcoming. Cultural and natural history by a gifted writer intimate with th park. Historic and scenic photographs, and personal perspectives by key figures in the park's history.

Kirk, Ruth. *Exploring Mount Rainier.* Seattle: University of Washington Press, 1968. A standby; an excellent visitor's guide to the park.

McNulty, Tim, and Pat O'Hara. *Mount Rainier National Park: Realm of the Sleeping Giant.* Del Mar, Calif.: Woodlands Press, 1985. Prose and photographs exploring the park's natural history.

Rohde, Jerry and Gisela. *Mount Rainier National Park: Tales, Trails, & Auto Tours.* McKinleyville, Calif.: MountainHome Books, 1996. A wonderfully detailed and historically informed driving and hiking guide to the park and nearby communities.

Schmoe, F. W. *Our Greatest Mountain.* New York: G. P. Putnam's Sons, 1925. An impressive early natural history by the park's first naturalist. (See also the author's *A Year in Paradise*)

Spring, Ira, and Harvey Manning. *50 Hikes in Mount Rainier National Park.* Seattle: The Mountaineers, 1988. The complete hiking guide to Mount Rainier's trails by two longtime experts.

Steelquist, Robert, and Pat O'Hara. *Traveler's Companion to Mount Rainier National Park.* Seattle: Northwest Interpretive Association, 1987. Beautifully illustrated touring guide to the park.

History

Carpenter, Cecelia Svinth. *Where the Waters Begin: The Traditional Nisqually Indian History of Mount Rainier.* Seattle: Northwest Interpretative Association, 1994. A sensitive history of the Nisqually people's long and intimate relationship with the mountain.

Catton, Theodore. *Wonderland: An Administrative History of Mount Rainier National Park.* Seattle: National Park Service Cultural Resources Program, 1996. A well-documented chronicle of the park during its first century. (Also see the author's "The Campaign to Establish Mount Rainier National Park,

142

Colophon

Composed by The
Mountaineers Books
using the font
Mrs. Eaves for text
and Trajan for
display lines.

THE MOUNTAINEERS, founded in 1906, is a non-profit outdoor activity and conservation club, whose mission is "to explore, study, preserve, and enjoy the natural beauty of the outdoors. . . ." Based in Seattle, Washington, the club is now the third-largest such organization in the United States, with 15,000 members and five branches throughout Washington State.

The Mountaineers sponsors both classes and year-round outdoor activities in the Pacific Northwest, which include hiking, mountain climbing, ski-touring, snowshoeing, bicycling, camping, kayaking and canoeing, nature study, sailing, and adventure travel. The club's conservation division supports environmental causes through educational activities, sponsoring legislation, and presenting informational programs. All club activities are led by skilled, experienced volunteers, who are dedicated to promoting safe and responsible enjoyment and preservation of the outdoors.

If you would like to participate in these organized outdoor activities or the club's programs, consider a membership in The Mountaineers. For information and an application, write or call The Mountaineers, Club Headquarters, 300 Third Avenue West, Seattle, Washington 98119; (206) 284-6310.

The Mountaineers Books, an active, nonprofit publishing program of the club, produces guidebooks, instructional texts, historical works, natural history guides, and works on environmental conservation. All books produced by The Mountaineers are aimed at fulfilling the club's mission.

Send or call for our catalog of more than 300 outdoor titles:

 The Mountaineers Books
1001 SW Klickitat Way, Suite 201
Seattle, WA 98134

1-800-553-4453

e-mail: mbooks@mountaineers.org

website: www.mountaineers.org

COLOPHON

Composed by The
Mountaineers Books
using the font
Mrs. Eaves for text
and Trajan for
display lincs.

THE MOUNTAINEERS, founded in 1906, is a non-profit outdoor activity and conservation club, whose mission is "to explore, study, preserve, and enjoy the natural beauty of the outdoors. . . ." Based in Seattle, Washington, the club is now the third-largest such organization in the United States, with 15,000 members and five branches throughout Washington State.

The Mountaineers sponsors both classes and year-round outdoor activities in the Pacific Northwest, which include hiking, mountain climbing, ski-touring, snowshoeing, bicycling, camping, kayaking and canoeing, nature study, sailing, and adventure travel. The club's conservation division supports environmental causes through educational activities, sponsoring legislation, and presenting informational programs. All club activities are led by skilled, experienced volunteers, who are dedicated to promoting safe and responsible enjoyment and preservation of the outdoors.

If you would like to participate in these organized outdoor activities or the club's programs, consider a membership in The Mountaineers. For information and an application, write or call The Mountaineers, Club Headquarters, 300 Third Avenue West, Seattle, Washington 98119; (206) 284-6310.

The Mountaineers Books, an active, nonprofit publishing program of the club, produces guidebooks, instructional texts, historical works, natural history guides, and works on environmental conservation. All books produced by The Mountaineers are aimed at fulfilling the club's mission.

Send or call for our catalog of more than 300 outdoor titles:

 The Mountaineers Books
1001 SW Klickitat Way, Suite 201
Seattle, WA 98134

1-800-553-4453
e-mail: mbooks@mountaineers.org
website: www.mountaineers.org